AGENDA

CONTENTS

G000114717

Editorial	4
Introduction: Patricia McCarthy	5
Norman Buller: A sequence of poems	9

ESSAYS, MEMOIRS, TRIBUTES

Henry Moore: Lullaby Sleeping Head, 1973 lithograph.
Part of a series illustrating Auden's poems — 13
Fjord, 1973 lithograph. Part of the same series — 14

Peter Mudford: The Memorableness of W.H. Auden – A Personal View — 15

Nigel Thompson: Extracts from a long poem
'To W.H. Auden in Heaven' and Note. — 23

Anita Money: Memories of my uncle, W.H. Auden, and of working
on *Agenda* — 32

Dylan Willoughby: Dusk at St. Marks, As Seen From Dunkin Donuts –
a poem inspired by Auden — 35

Patricia McCarthy: The Long Hurt of it:
a poem for W.H. Auden and Chester Kallman — 36

Rüdiger Görner: From Iceland to Kirchstetten – On W.H. Auden's
verbal Journeys — 37

John Greening: Bird Lore – a poem for Louis MacNeice — 44

Steven O'Brien: Scrying Stone – a poem for Louis MacNeice on Achill — 45

Peter McDonald: This mirror of wet sand – Louis MacNeice's Achill Poems — 46

Desmond O'Grady: Memories of Louis MacNeice and poem 'Reading
the Unpublished Manuscripts of Louis MacNeice at
Kinsale Harbour' — 58

Dennis O'Driscoll: a poem 'Michael Hamburger 1924 – 2007' — 60

Will Stone: Unpicked Apples: Memories of Michael Hamburger — 61

1

Wolfgang Görtschacher: Against Prejudice and Ignorance –
Michael Hamburger's Celebration of German
Literature in the United States   70

POEMS

Andrew Waterman: Happiness   85

Diana Brodie: Wedding Music   87
    Glass Heads   88

Nigel Jarrett: Nuptials   89
    Warrior   90

Dylan Willoughby: What Blossoms   91
    Old Growth   91

Greg Delanty: At my Mother's Bed   92
    A Small Prayer   93

Geraldine Paine: The unmarked grave   94

Anne Ryland: My Mother's Salt Coat   95

Wendy Robinson: Autolycus: Old Crow   96

Erinn Batykefer: Cicada Year   98
    Apple Family   98

Alex Smith: Hortyard   99
    Charlie Parker in Saffron Walden   102

Roger Elkin: Water Barrel   103

Chrys Salt: Lost   104

John White: Tullanee   105

John Powell Ward: Love   106

Susan Minish: Voyaging   107

Brendan McMahon: Owls   108
    Song   108

Chris Jones: Nevermas   109

John Gibbens: A Yellow Rose   111
    Dwellling   111

Roland John: The Old Ironworks   112
    The Collector   112

Sue Roe: Drawing a Peach 114
The Artist's Wife as a Young Girl 115

Will Stone: Harrowing 116

Kate Scott: All the men I've never slept with 117

Linda Benninghoff: August 118

Daniel Tobin: The Late Show 119

OBITUARY

W.S. Milne: Edward Lowbury, 1913-2007 120

LONG POEM

John Kinsella: Requiem 122

TWO CHOSEN BROADSHEET POETS

Caroline Clark: The Myth of the Nightingale 141
Tonight Moscow 142
Tale of Tales 142
Dacha 143

Adam Wyeth: Leland Bardwell 144
Carry the Torture 145
Chamber Music 146
Dad 147

NOTES FOR BROADSHEET POETS 10 148

BIOGRAPHIES 155

Henry Moore: Split Stone, 1973 lithograph 159
Divided Landscape, 1973 lithograph 160

Photographs on the front and back cover from rare family pictures of **Anita Auden** (Money) and her son, Otto.

Lithographs by **Henry Moore**, who was born in Castleford on 30th July, 1898, the son of a Yorkshire miner. After serving in the First World War, he studied drawing and sculpture at Leeds School of Art. From the late 1940s until his death he was recognised as the most celebrated and most controversial artist of his time. His reputation now speaks for itself. The lithographs printed in this issue (and other works online) are from a selection of Henry Moore's work on sale in the **Artco Gallery, Leeds**. Tel 0113 262 0056. Email: info@artco.co.uk Website: www.artco.co.uk

Editorial

Welcome to this issue of *Agenda*, **Lauds**, which is indeed one of praise or high commendation, focusing on W.H. Auden, Louis MacNeice, and Michael Hamburger. This issue also looks to the future, and our modern age, with, among other pieces, the long sequence by the prolific, energetic John Kinsella, and the excerpts from Nigel Thompson's 'A Letter to W.H. Auden'.

Many thanks to all the distinguished contributors – we are honoured to include some who knew and/or were related to the above poets personally – and to every subscriber and reader, all of whom give a vibrant interchange to a poetry journal such as this.

Thanks, also, to the Arts Council for their continuing support. A special tribute must be paid to the Po-shing Woo Foundation that has supported *Agenda* most generously for many years, and is now being closed down. Without the Po-shing Woo Foundation's support, *Agenda* would, at times, have been unable to continue. Its support has helped the magazine to flourish and become established in its renaissance.

With the Arts Council under increasing pressure to re-distribute and cut down its funding, it is vitally important for long-standing, highly-regarded magazines such as *Agenda* to maintain a healthy subscription list in order to survive. The equally long-standing and celebrated *London Magazine* (in which W.H. Auden had some poems published) has now had its Arts Council grant withdrawn, and this is a very sad and ominous sign of the times, as well as a serious loss for our national archive. Our sympathies go to Sebastian Barker, the Editor, who has had to step down after years of dedication, flair and very hard work.

Therefore, can I please ask you if you do have a subscription reminder with this issue, or if you have forgotten to re-subscribe, to do so as soon as possible to give *Agenda* the strength it needs for its stability and continuance.

Do not forget to look at the ever-expanding **website www.agendapoetry.co.uk** for online supplements (both poetry and paintings), **Broadsheets** for young poets and artists, news and other surprises. This gets updated after each issue comes out.

If you wish to check your subscription status, do email us at **www.agendapoetry. co.uk** and we will get back to you promptly.

Marcus Frederick   **Patricia McCarthy**

Future issues will include: A 50th Birthday issue for Greg Delanty, and general section, a Welsh issue, a General Anthology issue.

Introduction

This issue celebrates the centenary (2007) of two important poets, W.H. Auden (1907–1973) and Louis MacNeice (1907–1963), whose reputations now exceed the narrow definition of 'thirties poets'. Edward Mendelson, editor of *W.H Auden: Collected Poems* (Faber, revised edition, 2007) speaks of Auden as 'the most universal of modern poets' because he was 'the most individual'. Over the past three centuries, he claims, of poets who wrote in English, Auden's poems 'respond to the widest range of emotional and moral experience, and the widest range of diction and style'. Auden himself asserted that all his poems he had written for love: love of mankind, love of language, of poets, lovers. As Mendelson affirms: 'His poems bear witness to the close connection between intelligence and love'.

Despite his popular appeal among non-poetry lovers, even, with his poem 'Stop all the Clocks' towards the end of the film 'Four Weddings and a Funeral', he is frequently considered to be an obscure or inaccessible poet. However, in a letter to a friend, he explained how his autobiography is not required, since 'anything of importance that happens to one is immediately incorporated, however obscurely, in a poem'. As Mendelson points out, his obscurity was not that of expression but sometimes the hidden experience that provoked him to write the poem, although he would often insist on explaining that experience in prose many years later.

He was influenced by a whole history of English language poets, including Anglo Saxon (in his early work, and he made specific references to lines in Old English poems throughout his work), Langland, Milton, Dryden, Pope, Byron, Winthrop Mackworth Praed, Dickinson, Tennyson, Hopkins, Graves, and William Carlos Williams. In an interesting book, *Strange Likeness: The Use of Old English in Twentieth Century Poetry* (Oxford University Press, 2006), Chris Jones deals with the re-discovery of Anglo-Saxon by Pound, Auden, Edwin Morgan and Seamus Heaney. He summarises: 'To be a writer working through the Old English inheritance then, is to be something of an inner émigré, abroad in one's own tradition.' Jones suggests that Auden finds in Old English 'a strange likeness with the violence in his own century, often deploying the idiom he develops from Old English when writing of conflict' whether imaginary (e.g. 'Paid on both Sides'), historical (e.g. 'The Age of Anxiety') or connected to sexual anxiety. Jones interprets 'The Wanderer' as 'a coming-out narrative contingent on understanding several allusions that Auden makes to Old English poems' with his simultaneous strategy of concealment and disclosure. Auden, in turn, of course, went on to influence many English and American poets who came after him.

In his wonderfully thorough, rigorous and comprehensive, very readable reference book, *W.H. Auden: A Commentary* (Faber 2007 pbck. published for the Auden Centenary year, 613 pages), poet and scholar John Fuller admits 'There are limits to one man's understanding of a polymath such as Auden.' However, in this edition, revised in 1998, that Fuller calls ' a book that you look things up in', not to be read at one sitting, Fuller manages to encompass the publishing history, paraphrases, difficult passages, drafts, sources and influences of Auden's corpus of poetry, with illuminating notes on the poems as well as critical appreciation. Auden's formal and intellectual range is established as being on a par with that of Yeats and Eliot, and his particular interests – psychological, philosophical, anthropological, theological, political and historical – which are explained all help the reader to understand this complex poet. For readers who feel, like Benjamin Britten who collaborated with Auden on song-cycles and libretti, 'a bad inferiority complex in the company of brains like Wystan Auden', and for those seeking further insights, this companion single volume is a must.

Agenda has a very special link with Wystan Auden in that his niece, Anita Auden (Money), whose memories of her uncle appear here, herself a scholar at St. Hughes, Oxford, worked for many years on *Agenda* with the founder editor, William Cookson. It is an honour, also, to have an essay on Wystan, suffused with personal memories, by Peter Mudford who was married to another niece of Auden, Rita Auden, Anita's sister, who very sadly died earlier this month. A second essay, by Rüdiger Görner, takes an unusual perspective on the poet, analysing his own particular music and showing his links with Austria.

Peter McDonald, the well-known poet and essayist whose essay 'The Irish MacNeice' appears in this issue of *Agenda*, edited the *Collected Poems of Louis MacNeice* specially published by Faber last year for MacNeice's centenary. In his Introduction, McDonald shows that, like Auden, MacNeice transcends the label of a 'thirties' poet. McDonald demonstrates the problems and responsibilities involved in editing a Collected Poems, some of these being that a poet is not necessarily the best judge of his own work, and that the work of MacNeice (like that of Auden, and of poets in general) was uneven.

In the new paperback edition (Faber 2007), originally published in 1988, of Louis MacNeice's *Selected Poems*, edited by Michael Longley, the introductory essay by Longley is an illuminating and succinct appraisal of MacNeice. Longley shows his work as a struggle of light to conquer the dark, of the poet as an outsider, not just in his native Ulster, but everywhere, neither 'Free of all roots nor yet a rooted peasant', always displaced as he bore witness to the contemporary world, producing 'A turning page of shine and sound, the day's maze'. Longley points out that 'this selection favours the lyrical MacNeice', who 'gets inside words', and adds 'Seldom can the lyric have carried so much freight and remained airborne'. In his later poems, too, where MacNeice succeeds in using verse as he defined it, as a 'precision instrument', the lyric poem, according to Longley, 'reaches a new frontier'. His work explores all that means to be human, both publicly and privately, with catalogues, spirals, and exhilarating imagery and forms, so much so that Longley mentions him in the same breath as Yeats, attributing to both poets a special 'zest' and 'leaping vitality'. This bursts forth particularly in Part IV of *Autumn Journal* where MacNeice proclaims:

> I must pursue this life, it will not be only
> A drag from numbered stone to numbered stone
> But a ladder of angels, river turning tidal.

Who would not want to be the woman who 'left my walls/Dancing over and over with her shadow,/Whose hair is entwined in all my waterfalls'?

It is interesting to read MacNeice's unfinished autobiography, *The Strings are False*, which was also reprinted by Faber last year to coincide with the centenary, and which contains a New Preface by Derek Mahon. As Mahon states, 'Terence Brown (*Louis MacNeice: Sceptical Vision*, 1975) was one of the first to point out that there is much more to the poet than the well-known "surface brilliance"'. MacNeice's philosophical development – which, according to Brown, goes back to Heraclitus, river in spate, the living moment and 'incarnate existence' – seems to be as significant as that of Auden.

There is no doubt that MacNeice went through dry periods such as the poems in *Ten Burnt Offerings* and *Autumn Sequel* (unlike the 'magnificent marathon' of *Autumn Journal*) which Auden, along with Longley, found 'a bit dull'. As Longley says, in the latter collections 'the tensions between light and darkness were too even', for MacNeice was a 'poet of the solstice, of the uneven and unbalancing pull, at his best in his twenties and thirties and again after his fiftieth birthday'.

Both Auden and MacNeice came from privileged backgrounds, both went to public school, followed by Oxford, yet both had instabilities that undermined them, but which at the same time gave an edge to their poems. MacNeice had many affairs and a drink problem; Auden seemed to suffer perpetual heartbreak since meeting Chester Kallman. This was offset by the problems of being a homosexual at a time when homosexuality was illegal. In different ways, then, both poets, as outsiders, were caught up in dualistic dichotomies, in conflicts between public and private worlds, between nightmare and dream, between survival and anarchic despair, between love and its loss, between loyalty and betrayal, between fragmentation and psychic wholeness, between public acceptance and attack. Both liked to think of themselves as having been caught up in the Spanish Civil War, and both can be criticised for their lack of involvement in the second world war, and yet their awareness of it – Auden disappeared to the U.S. and MacNeice only returned from the U.S. because he thought he was 'missing a bit of history'. Auden, in fact, was so out of favour with the establishment that he was even accused erroneously of being an Axis spy. Nevertheless, the dualities added to the composite ideal of what Longley calls 'the poet as all rounder' who includes philosophy, politics, classical and popular culture in his poetry. Auden, at some point, praised this 'binocular vision' and commented that 'one fallible symptom of greatness is its double focus.' Poetry might well 'make nothing happen', but through poetry and life 'We must love one another or die'.

It is interesting to note that both Auden and MacNeice became friends, wrote poems to one another, wrote a long, joint 'Last Will and Testament', and collaborated on a sequence of poems: *Letters from Iceland*. When MacNeice suddenly died in 1963, in Auden's moving elegy, 'The Cave of Making', Auden speaks directly to Louis, his 'dear Shade':

7

how much, in our lonely dens, we need the companionship
   of our good dead, to give us
comfort on dowly days when the self is a nonentity
   dumped on a mound of nothing,
to break the spell of our self-enchantment when lip-smacking
   imps of mawk and hooey
write with us what they will...

*

The above quotation could also apply to the revered poet, translator and essayist, Michael Hamburger, whom this issue also honours. Michael died at the beginning of this year and was long associated with and a contributor to *Agenda*.

The Agenda office will miss opening his poems and translations tapped out faintly on an old typewriter with a worn ribbon, and his letters on their flimsy paper, his distinctive handwriting formed by the thin-nib of his pen or biro. In the last year or so before he died, he was working hard on his own poems and earnestly desired to be best known as a poet in his own right rather than as a translator. This issue pays tribute to the man and the translator. Future issues will focus on his poetry.

*

Agenda is honoured to print the long poem 'Requiem' by John Kinsella in this issue. Kinsella represents a significant voice for the here and now, and for the future. Auden would surely have praised him for his huge perspectives and 'binocular vision' which make for 'symptoms of greatness'.

All the poets in this issue, and those celebrated, would probably agree with John Kinsella in his latest book, *Disclosed Poetics* (Manchester University Press), who simply states, 'I make poems' and honestly admits, 'I cannot place art above anything outside itself.' He defines the lyric as being 'a representational grounding of time' and speaks of the inseparability of 'the singing of a poem, the speaking of a poem, the rhythm and intonation of a poem'. He refers to the book as a whole as 'not an analysis, but a stretching out of the poetic line. It is commentary, but interactive commentary'. It is hoped that this issue of *Agenda* manages, like his book, to be a 'conversation between text, reader, place and poet'.

Let us agree with Auden, then, about the educative function of art, and its possible moral power. Let us endorse, too, the two kinds of art that Auden went on to define: 'escape-art', which all men need, and 'parable-art' which, in Auden's words, 'shall teach man to unlearn hatred and learn love'.

Laudemus.

Patricia McCarthy

Norman Buller

A Sequence

Aboriginal

Some time ago she had erected fences
for fear of raiders
riding to the rim of neighbouring heights,
bent on invasion.

Marriage and its yield she'd staked about her
like a stockade
that she to casual Lotharios
would be impregnable.

But silently, from deep in her defences,
a figure rises,
native to the land on which she'd settled,
so long forgotten,

the aboriginal, once more emerging
above his bondage
to take her on his breast and set her free
with irresistible possession.

Cage Bird

He came upon her
from a songless region.

He listened for her
but could hear only
panic of caged feathers
fearing escape
and shrilled mockery.

What longing,
what fraught need
did she suppress
jailed in her phantom self?

Beating at insubstantial bars,
her wings
cast an untouchable sorrow
over his life.

Simple Things

If he could go to her for simple things,
forgetting misery and pain,
though these are simple too, and must remain,

he would return to strife
not stronger but more willing to endure
barren complexities of war,

being certain of one further solaced hour,
tender and unfolding as a flower.

Absent in a Library

Casually, in some book,
he reads 'She had her lover until dawn'
and instantly their spectral limbs convulse,
ghost mouths bind, cavern-searching.

Strange how these unfleshed words
pipe nameless bloods
through the mind's arteries;
transfuse to him
a passion he can name
with their two phantom selves;
flooding him with this fever
despite exile.

The History Lesson

His voice, like a recorded noise,
relates by rote textbook careers
of kings and rebels, passing like
a threadless needle through ghost boys.

In treason's image she returns,
severed from him more tellingly
by ancient execution than
the concrete miles' reality.

He drones about the rights of man
and how in him a reign ago
she gave them credence wondrously,
so saved his state from overthrow...

Young boys learn kings are toppled, how
a queen becomes the rebels' whore.
He gropes among the broken crowns
to find the symbol that they wore.

Breaking Stone

Turn from her!

Only a man
blind as a stone
would reach for her hand.

Her carnal loveliness
shimmers and breaks
as his hand
breaks her surface.

Yet only a man
stone blind and mad
would

turn from her.

That Converse Pain

Into his side she grows,
a thorn far more compelling
than the unfurling rose.

No woman born
can bring man only beauty
but bestows

that converse pain
she learned when torn
from Adam's bone.

Lullaby Sleeping Head, 1973 lithograph frm W.H. Auden poems/Moore Lithographs. One of a selection of Henry Moore's lithographs for sale in the Artco Gallery, Leeds. Tel 0113 262 0056. Website www.artco.co.uk Reproduced by kind permission of The Henry Moore Foundation and of the Artco Gallery.

AP 8/10   Moore

Fjord, 1973 lithograph. Reproduced by kind permission of The Henry Moore Foundation and of the Artco Gallery, Leeds.

Peter Mudford

This article is dedicated to the memory of Wystan's niece,
Rita Auden 22 August 1942 – 3 January 2008

The Memorableness of W.H. Auden

A Personal View

The evenings when Wystan came to dinner were always memorable. I am thinking of the years between 1961 and 1973 when he came to dinner with his family in London. He had completed his years as Professor of Poetry at Oxford where his lectures remained among the most memorable parts of my Oxford education. He spent his winters in New York, and his summers in Kirchstetten, Austria, in the only house he ever owned.

On his way through London he always came to have dinner with John, his older brother and Sheila, his wife, with their daughters Anita and Rita, to whom he was devoted, and myself as Rita's husband at the time. These dinners were very much family occasions; and as with all family reunions not without their tensions. Wystan enjoyed them because of his affection for a family he did not have, and because this was a place where the public figure, his face recognised wherever he went, could become entirely the private man. Such tensions as there were arose only through differences in temperament, and paths through life of a very different kind.

John's career, working for the Geological Survey of India, mapping the Himalayas, visiting the areas hit by earthquakes and advising on the construction of dams, had been one of great scientific distinction. He was modest, reticent and deeply civilised. His wife, Sheila, was well-known in India as an artist. We all loved her paintings, which hung on the walls, particularly the 'The Donkey Race': the races take place across a barren plain against a backdrop of dark Himalayan peaks.

They were both people of great warmth of heart for their family, and for Wystan. But it had not always been easy to be known as the relatives of 'the great poet'. On these evenings, one could not entirely forget the unevenness with which fame distributes its rewards. Sheila with her unfailing humour was known to murmur before them: 'I do not like poetry!'

Families who meet at irregular intervals do not talk about high-minded things. I once got a sharp look for mentioning a new production of *Lohengrin* which I thought good. Sheila enjoyed cooking for someone who thought statues should be put up for great chefs, and Wystan, who always arrived punctually at six for his martinis, brought with him laughter, with irritation at times, concerning every-day things, and gossip about mutual friends. The local and the particular sometimes ranged into the universal. On one occasion, he was especially delighted by Martin Gardner's *The Ambidextrous Universe* (1964) which provided the scientific evidence for Nature having a 'left-handed twist.'

Wystan was magisterial, authoritative, and could be dismissive; but he was also, unlike many with public reputations, a very good listener. Here, as it were, in the interval between two notes of music, one felt in the presence of genius. Elsewhere he has talked about his ability to write poetry as 'a gift' and this gift expressed itself, too, in the feeling given in his company of being in touch with what is common to humanity. He understood. He could be irritating too, and as he complained of Yeats, 'silly like us,' asserting, for example, that no one could dream in colour. But beyond that, Wystan did have another super-sensory power of being right, rooted in modesty, and never far away from laughter, or seriousness. He could be, as he once described Lord Byron, 'the master of the airy manner.'

The memorableness I have been describing here is that of a very public man on private occasions. This centenary year of his birth has rightly been celebrated with readings, talks, and television programmes about his work and life. In many, the same stories about him are retold and the discussion of his homosexuality, (there really is a limit to what can be said) and his foibles are given as much prominence as his poems. Inevitably, and rightly, there has been much discussion of the relative merits of his early and later works, and of his longer works, 'The Orators', 'New Year Letter', and 'The Age of Anxiety'. These works often cannot be understood without hard work, knowledge of his allusions and reflection. This is true of much great art. It is not to be siphoned up like drinking through a straw.

Wystan once defined poetry as 'memorable speech.' There are great complete poems, but there are also huge chunks of his poetry, in both his long and his shorter works, which are not memorable, even when re-read. Not just because the meaning and the allusions can be obscure, but because there does not seem to be an inevitable connection between rhythm and meaning, which alone makes poetry memorable.

And yet there is another Auden, a portable, remembered Auden, whose lines sound and resound in the inner-ear, like phrases in music, summoned up unpredictably, spontaneously, as one goes about daily life and which offer a commentary, consolation, often joy. His most famous poem is perhaps 'In Praise of Limestone' and though it is to be admired as a whole, the central section seems to me 'unmemorable' while the last three lines, once inscribed, are never to be forgotten…

> when I try to imagine a faultless love,
> Or the life to come, what I hear is the murmur
> Of underground streams, what I see is a limestone landscape.

Here, Auden has something in common with Shakespeare's 'memorable speech,' a language purged of everything except simplicity. In a performance of Shakespeare's plays, the number of lines which sound and resound never ceases to astonish. How memorable they are, even outside their context! We carry with us lines and phrases which are reactivated as defences against daily life, because they have entered our vocabulary of feeling, like friends met unexpectedly in the street. This is especially true for me of Auden, in a variety of ways.

In the 1700 lines of 'New Year Letter', for example, what I value most is this:

> Whenever I begin to think
> About the human creature we
> Must nurse to sense and decency,
> An English area comes to mind,
> I see the native of my kind
> As a locality I love.
> The limestone moors that stretch from *Brough*
> To *Hexham* and the *Roman Wall*,
> There is my symbol of us all.

In what follows I do not want to make special claims for lines which have an affirmative power for me. Others will make their own quite different selection. But with Auden, they fall for me under certain headings, or they form a particular pattern which relates them in many cases to larger themes. I do not know the area which meant so much to him in the lines from 'New Year Letter' but the lines resonate with a feeling for England as place and landscape. Here, as in the opening of

> Look, stranger on this island now
> The leaping light for your delight discovers

where the chalk cliffs oppose the 'pluck and knock' of the tide, the lines shape the contours of feeling about this island. They come back to me whenever returning.

Friendship and its very different partner, love, form the core of many of his finest poems and they are seen in many different guises.

> Now north and south and east and west
> Those I love lie down to rest;
> The moon looks on them all...

The poem does not just express what we would have liked to express but could not: it becomes a mine for keeping alive our feelings and our passions. Lines like these become absorbed into consciousness.

It is striking how many of his poems are written for friends, the inscription of whose names at the start sound a particular note, in the knowledge that what follows would give them pleasure: 'Come when you can, your room will be ready.' In writing a poem for friends, whether those who had influenced him intellectually, like Friedrich Heer or like Liebe Frau Emma , his housekeeper in Austria, he was acknowledging a debt . Poetry became a form of thanks-giving, and well-wishing. Wystan, as man and poet inherited the aura of the white Magus. 'New Year Letter' is dedicated to Elizabeth Mayer,

> But always there are such as you
> Forgiving, helping what we do.

He did not forget that, when twenty years later, he commemorated her again after a visit to an 'old people's home.'

Wit was never long absent from his conversation, or his poetry for friends, as in his poem for the Russian composer, Nicholas Nabokov:

> The trees encountered on a country stroll
> Reveal a lot about that country's soul.

But the aphoristic sharpness is not constrained by the personal context.

Equally, his sense of loss on the death of friends succeeds in giving elegy a poignance which we can share, as in the poem, 'The Cave of Making' for Louis MacNeice, 'lover of women and Donegal.' What he has lost is not just the presence of someone who long ago joined him on 'The journey to Iceland' and who would have relished having the boundary of the Holy Roman Empire pointed out to him, but someone who also knew poetry was an 'unpopular art' which could not be 'turned into background noise for study.' It 'stubbornly insists on being read or ignored':

> I wish you hadn't
> Caught that cold, but the dead we miss are easier
> to talk to.

The un-emphatic conversational rhythm matches what is being said, and lingers in the mind as a way of coming to terms with other deaths.

In the poems dedicated to friends, which are also about interests shared in friendship, Wystan takes as themes things which have stillness and permanence: the rooms in a house, the features of a landscape: woods, mountains, lakes, islands, streams.

This sense of stillness and permanence is completely absent from his poems about love, which are not written for individuals, with the exception of 'Tell me the truth about love,' written for Hedli Anderson, Louis MacNeice's future wife. She was a singer, and the poem is a blues song. This, like the other love poems, is riddled by Time. They are poems about love which is not gendered. About his private life, Wystan was private. Although in later years, his loneliness became increasingly apparent, he never alluded to it. He asked the recipients of his letters to destroy them, and did not wish his biography to be written. He talked about what interested or dismayed him, but never about himself.

The love poetry is often celebratory and admonitory:

> Certainty, fidelity
> On the stroke of midnight pass...

It is realistic:

> My dear one is mine
> As mirrors are lonely...

And undaunted:

> To fresh defeats he still must move
> To further griefs and greater
> And the defeat of grief.

Aware of the assurances which cannot be given:

> Perhaps the roses really want to grow
> The vision seriously intends to stay
> If I could tell you I would let you know.

It may be said that some of these lines come from poems which are not just poems about love and that suggests why they remain memorable and available to us, beyond the circumstances which gave rise to them.

Much in his love poetry alludes both to erotic joy and its impermanence:

> I'll love you, dear, I'll love you
> Till China and Africa meet,
> And the river jumps over the mountain
> And the salmon sing in the street.

These lines from 'One Evening,' a poem that is flawless, are uttered only to be followed by the warning:

> O let not time deceive you,
> You cannot conquer time...
> Into many a green valley
> Drifts the appalling snow...
> ... And the crack in the tea-cup opens
> A lane to the land of the dead...

Nonetheless:

> ... Life remains a blessing
> Although you cannot bless.

The whole poem is memorable, but it contains lines such as these which flow back into consciousness as a commentary on circumstances of many different kinds. The memorable nature of the language comes from the ease with which it can be translated from one situation to another, liberated from the context of the poem as a whole. This does not diminish the whole poem but enhances it, as happens with Shakespeare. Many of his poems relate to the ways in which 'weeping anarchic Aphrodite' (who mourns for the death of Sigmund Freud) orchestrates our inner lives, and the fevers to which they are subject as a result of betrayal, and unreciprocated feeling. We want to be loved alone, but:

> If equal affection cannot be
> Let the more loving one be me.

Because the feeling is objective and impersonal, it relates to the human condition, not to his personal predicament. Unlike Donne's love poetry, it lacks self-dramatisation, without becoming impersonal. The 'verbal contraption' of the poem always has someone inside it.

Every poet helps us to map our personal landscapes in particular ways. With Auden as a poet of the thirties, this inevitably has to do with politics, but not with the politics of his period only. His voice remains memorable because it expresses what we would often prefer to forget:

> To save your world, you asked this man to die
> Would this man, if he saw you now, ask why?

A world where children grow up without hearing:

> Of any world where promises were kept
> Or one could weep because another wept.

Of the power of the unexceptional individual to cause limitless death and destruction:

> Clutching a little case
> He walks out briskly to infect a city
> Whose terrible future may have just arrived.

He reminds us of a change which has occurred since 1945:

> We shan't, not since Stalin and Hitler
> trust ourselves ever again: we know that, subjectively,
> all is possible.

Of what has not changed:

>And the living nations wait
>Each sequestered in its hate.

And the vast inequalities of wealth which separate the rich from the poor:

>Nor ask what doubtful act allows
>Our freedom in this English house
>Our picnics in the sun.

Or the feeling of threat and menace which throbs in the modern world:

>O what is that sound which so thrills the ear
>Down in the valley drumming, drumming?

And the destruction we are likely to bring on ourselves by our own aggression:

>Those to whom evil is done
>Do evil in return.

Lines like these become inscribed on memory because like the Chorus in a Greek play, they offer a commentary on our time. And they do not belong to one period of his creative life, to the 'English' or the 'American' Auden.

At family reunions, poetry was never discussed, and scarcely mentioned, except one evening when Wystan recited with great relish from his volume of *Academic Graffiti*, in that voice once described as being 'like the gin running out in the bath-water.'

>When the young Kant
>Was told to kiss his aunt,
>He obeyed the Categorical Must,
>But only just.

But in his conversation he was often cautionary: 'I don't think you should do that, my dear' and sometimes aphoristic, as in much of his poetry:

>   …weather
>Is what nasty people are
>Nasty about and the nice
>Show a common joy in observing

Or:

> Though one cannot always
> Remember exactly why one has been happy,
> There is no forgetting that one was.

In spite of his Christian faith, he did not talk about religion unless to explain why the Manichees were wrong; but in his presence one was aware of someone who strove, sometimes a little desperately, to show 'an affirming flame.' It was part of the job of a poet, the occupation he insisted on having in his passport, to 'bless what there is for being,' and as he said in his great poem on the death of W.B Yeats, 'in the prison of his days/ Teach the free man how to praise.' The first phrase commemorates him on the tablet in Christ Church Cathedral, the second in Westminster Abbey. In spite of the word 'teach' and he was often school-masterly, his humility taught him that 'poetry makes nothing happen, it survives…a way of happening, a mouth,' in a world where we have 'no means of learning what is really going on.'

He leaves a poetic language which often comes very close to music where, as Wordsworth said, 'we murder to dissect' and where to ask what it means is to diminish it. It remains available as part of an inner song:

> Altogether elsewhere, vast
> Herds of reindeer move across
> Miles and miles of golden moss,
> Silently and very fast.
> …And the high green hill sits always by the sea…

As with all poetry, lines like these are 'for solitude, for company.'

Nigel Thompson

Note on 'To W.H. Auden in Heaven'

'To W.H. Auden in Heaven' attempts a homage to Auden in the master's own style, taking as its model the 'Letter to Lord Byron', which Auden wrote for the travel book *Letters from Iceland*, published with Louis MacNeice in 1937 after the two had spent the previous summer there. It is a typically anti-heroic epistle, the genesis of which Auden says occurred as 'I'd caught a heavy cold at Akureyri/And lunch was late and life was rather dreary.' In fact, Auden took a copy of Byron for the trip and had the brilliant idea of using Byron's offhand and chatty manner for a poem that would ostensibly fulfil the obligation to his publisher while allowing him the scope to observe a multitude of other topics. He wanted 'a form that was large enough to swim in/And talk on any subject that I choose,/From natural scenery to men and women,/Myself, the arts, the European news', but chose rime royal (from Chaucer's *Troilus and Criseyede*) rather than Byron's ottava rima. But, like Byron, he treated the stanza with loving disrespect and filled it with delightful romps through his views on life and literature in order to update Byron on what had happened since he died. With typical bravura Auden declares:

> Every exciting letter has enclosures,
> And so shall this – a bunch of photographs,
> Some out of focus, some with wrong exposures,
> Press cuttings, gossip, maps, statistics, graphs;
> I don't intend to do the thing by halves.
> I'm going to be very up to date indeed.
> It is a collage that you're going to read.

The selections published here show something of the scope of 'To W.H. Auden in Heaven'. It is in four sections, 163 stanzas of rime royal as compared with Auden's 159. Auden's poem was indeed a collage (mainly tending to the literary) where the present work attempts clearer divisions into today's manners, mores and conflicts, as the selections from Section I show. Sections II and III offer more comment on developments in politics, society, science and the arts. The final section (IV) – given here in full – follows Auden's poem in its short autobiographical sketch of the poet.

Extracts from

To W. H. Auden in Heaven

A Letter in his Centenary Year

Part I

'Dear Wystan' is the way I should begin
This letter to you, but today I fear
It may seem offhand or ungenuine.
'Dear Auden' is archaic, even 'dear'
These days is taken to be too sincere,
Unless you mean it. No wish to offend,
But could you take the first as from a friend?

Not that we ever met, although we crossed
Paths once in Ilkley by its windswept moor
The year you passed away and, yes, I tossed
Away the opportunity, too poor
To pay to hear you read. It was a bore.
But then a local adage urging 'sup all'
Persuaded me to pub-crawl with Jeff Nuttall.

Please, Wystan, overlook this sin of youth.
I know, it's inexcusable to miss
A maestro's reading and I was uncouth
(An ignorance that sadly brought no bliss),
Though happily a metamorphosis
Occurred and if I am still drinking hard
It is no longer with the avant-garde…

*

So now let's start the fun here, rock and roll,
        Break open all the bottles and get sloshed,
And if my measures do lack some control,
        Then who would notice? Thus my hands are washed.
        But in this letter to you, nothing's quashed,
It comes with all the news that's fit to hear.
There's mountains of it. Got your mountain gear?

*

24

So first, you want the good news or the bad?
    There's global warming, climate havoc, war
From Dafur to the suburbs of Baghdad
    And not a great deal to be hopeful for...
    Before we go through that particular door
Perhaps we should kick off with a surprise:
The whole world has gone mad for enterprise.

Yes, with the Eastern Bloc for driving force
    In '89 came Communism's end,
The Soviets reluctantly, of course,
    But Velvet Revolutions set the trend
    And party leaders reaped the dividend.
Perhaps the Russian mafia puts on airs,
But then why not? They're multibillionaires!

The Federation has its sister states,
    Each hoping for an upturn from decline,
A president who seldom delegates,
    Would never put dissenters down a mine,
    But manages to make them all incline
To one opinion. It looks autocratic
To Western minds. For them, it's democratic.

With aging Soviet missiles all kaput,
    The Cold War safe as history, now there's oil
To field as economic weapon, shut
    Supply off to a client less than loyal,
    And make a better deal on foreign soil:
With power in the pipeline, there are those
Who have a godlike power to dispose.

Out in the Far East, it's a different story.
    The year you died, I think saw Vietnam
Fall. For America there was no glory,
    But then Red China courted Uncle Sam
    And in a decade with designs, a dam
Or two, its output grew and now supplies
Computers, sportswear, toys and print silk ties.

The Yellow River's under yellow smog,
    Its factories a throwback to the scene
Your childhood Midlands had and now they hog
        The markets, too. The Dragon may be green
        With dollars, but there's little landscape seen:
In Northern Provinces, it's touch and go
Where coal dust carpets Shanxi's Gerzhuotou.

*

I write this from a bed-sit in the sticks
    Today and yes, like yours, it's warm and snug
But make this survey of world politics
        While feeling like a bug squashed in a rug
        On every side of which there is a tug
Of war. My intro starts on this, you see,
News of a *New* Age of Anxiety.

If there's anxiety, it's caused by change,
    Acceleration East and West is fast,
Increased mobility means we exchange
        The goods and services that used to last
        More rapidly, but change comes with a blast,
Less job security, less loyalty,
But bigger bonus, twice the royalty.

Where ideology is at an end,
    And thoughts are nothing new, but only clones
Of pluralistic freedom, now the trend
        Is working all your waking hours like drones
        Not for the State this time, but for the loans
To bolster national productivity,
Be it the GNP or GDP.

And yet we move about the world in droves
    From economic migrants, refugees,
Backpackers on a gap year from the groves
        Of Academe to businessmen who please
        Themselves where they will set up overseas.
The world we live in is transposable
And, like its products, all disposable.

*

Part IV

So time runs out and urges me to close,
    Not having taken too much of it up,
I trust. And as for other readers, those
    Brave two or three prepared to take the cup,
    The saucer and the biscuit – even sup –
My heartfelt thanks; and also to the stanza
For kindly housing this extravaganza.

I left you in a travesty of March
    And who knows what will really come this spring...
I dare say we will recognize the larch
    And other leafy denizens that bring
    Relief to skylines, sheltering birds that sing
And... Ah, Romantics made you feel neuralgic,
But then they sometimes make me turn nostalgic...

When all you had to do to be a poet
    Was charge about the English countryside,
Inspired if you could gather seed and sow it
    And hook a country maiden for a bride...
    Then ten young children whom you must provide
For? Come to think of it, the Modern Age
Is better than it looks upon the page.

But what of me? O Wystan, I'd be flattered
    To think that you had really meant to ask.
It's not as if a poet ever mattered
    (Well, not like you), but it's a simple task.
    And so with your *nil obstat* let me bask
A moment in historical reflection,
That is, if I have any recollection.

My grandfathers did well in cotton, lost
    The lot and therefore made no great impression
Upon the nation's wealth. It was the cost
    Of living through what was the Great Depression,
    Which passed you by, as you had a profession.
My parents were, like yours, at best ill matched.
The house we lived in small, semi-detached.

A prototype of comprehensive school
Fostered the basic skills, if nothing more
Than how to stop a nose bleed, break a rule
Or two – or even hide out in a store
Room during trig; the rest was Elsinore,
Revenge and tragedy were engineered
Within the A stream, but the E was feared.

If put on track as an economist,
Geology meant that I could take a trip
To Iceland, thus I braved the Northern mist,
Volcanic deserts, braided rivers, drip
Of rain, and took along for fellowship
Your 'Letter to Lord Byron'. As a guide
To glaciers its success was qualified.

My other book was *Crime and Punishment*,
A strange choice at the age of seventeen,
But very good for reading in a tent
Or in a cabin if the sea's serene;
Not that there was much time to read between
Rock breaking and the field geology
Siberian in its topology.

Too commonsensical or passionate,
I passed up on a university
The first time round and, as a drop-out, ate
The bitter fruit of my perversity;
(Not understanding its diversity)
Was postman, dustman, man that cut the grass,
And ended up in Italy, second class;

Then courtesy of R. and E. B. Browning,
Inhabited the flat at Casa Guidi
During the years when Italy was drowning
In violence, terrorism and quite needy
Of some stability; if it was seedy,
As a writer I enjoyed my first success
With several pieces for the *TLS*.

And then to Oxford, where I had my fill
Of scholarship, a doctorate too late
To benefit, and so – MA, D.Phil –
What could I do but, like you, educate?
But how the modern theorists loved to hate
A medievalist – me for a start –
Despite my reading Derrida and Barthes!

Eventually, of course, I got the push.
A college lecturer with no tenure fails
To keep a grip on things, lost in the rush
For honours, publications, but the scales
May tip back in my favour. It entails
Good fortune and the patronage of friends.
Of course, a letter may bring dividends.

So back in my Bohemia, I write this:
An open letter asking for no cash,
Perhaps a little credit up in bliss,
That's all. No matter if a cheque should flash
Before my eyes in payment as I dash
This off, it comes to you wrapped in rime royal,
With you for glitter and me as the foil.

But then, like me, you were the Suffering Man,
Although for you a Suffering Sphinx would be
More apt. How much you would have loved to swan
About the salons, perfect at a tea,
Pontificating to it beautifully
On love! At first, with Housman, yours was more
Than something fraught with violence and the poor.

(Oh, by the way, a footnote for you – now
I know it's way beyond its sell by date –
But this is not the breaking news or Dow
Jones daily average, but yet of late
As poet of love you met a better fate
On film and though it is unusual
Starred in *Four Weddings and a Funeral*.)

A democratic leveller in verse,
Perhaps Postmodernist before its time
You deftly mingled ballad metres, terse
Reflections, highbrow terms and bawdy rhyme
With registers that turned round on a dime.
And here the blame cannot be television,
More your antipathy to vatic vision.

You could not stand the Lakeland Poets or Keats,
Although we know you had a softer spot
For Byron – whether this was for his feats
Of versifying could be true or not –
But possibly his vices made you hot.
No doubt for doing what was not allowed
He left the country underneath a cloud.

Perhaps you felt some sympathy with this?
And whether led by innocence or guile
– Or was the Promised Land just promised bliss? –
But in America you lived in style,
The loft flat of a Greenwich Village pile.
I guess you hoped that here you could begin
Again in language turning mandarin.

But we admire the bulk of what you wrote,
In love or out, upon these Saxon shores;
The rest becomes a little more remote:
I find 'In Praise of Limestone' rather bores
Me… What about the *mezzogiorno* whores?
If cheap, at least, they could be colourful,
While limestone at its best is very dull.

In your day it was fine to mention 'pylon',
Indeed, it came to be thought *de rigeur,*
Although there was a sticking point with 'nylon',
Which all of you regarded with hauteur,
Perhaps it seemed to be less him more *her…*
We had to wait for Skylon and the New
Elizabethan Age when Larkin's crew

Could wallow *en abîme* in the demotic,
    When swearing generally came to be allowed,
As long as it was purely anecdotic –
    Something that you would hear among a crowd
    Of chaps, perhaps. At first, you know, it wowed
Us silly; now we've wallowed in the muck,
We exercise a little nip and tuck.

Love gave no inspiration – it is said –
    Or no distinctive rapture made you odd
Like some of those Romantics, but the head
    Too firmly ruled the heart and made you plod,
    A puritan who's hard work ethic God
Would have approved. Now in your other world,
I hope you sit ecstatic, wings unfurled.

Your poetry of prayer and vision, hope
    In something better for humanity,
And pedagogic patience had us cope
    And helped us all retain our sanity
    Despite the world, its chaos and its vanity.
So let us chorus with a rousing voice
And toast the poet who taught us to rejoice!

If you would pray for us while strumming hymns
    Upon your old celestial Joanna,
Pausing to sip ambrosial-style Pimm's
    After one's best camp Noel Coward manner,
    We should be grateful, gladly raise the banner
Again for you another hundred years
From now. But in the meantime, Wystan, cheers!

Anita Money (née Auden)

Memories of my uncle, W.H. Auden, and of working on *Agenda*

My background has a bearing on *Agenda* where I worked with William Cookson, the founding editor, for several years. My uncle Wystan (W.H. Auden) was close to my father, his brother, John, a geologist who worked for The Geological Survey of India (of which he was Director over the transition to Indian Independence) and later for the FAO (The Food and Agricultural arm of the United Nations) based in Rome. He had climbed in the Himalayas and was a founder member of the Himalayan Club. Wystan dedicated *The Ascent of F6* to him, the title inspired by K2 in the Karakoram. My mother Sheila Bonnerjee was a painter and came from a Bengali Calcutta family. She and two of her sisters, Anila (who also ended her days at Meadbank where Rachel, William Cookson's mother, had been and was taken on short excursions to the Café Rouge by my sister Rita) and Minnie, married Englishmen while another sister, Indira, married a Parsee. The two brothers, Protap and Bharat, neither of whom married, had been sent to school in England. Their grandfather, W.C Bonnerjee, or Grey Beard, as the family used to refer to him, was the first president of The Indian National Congress (in its early stages planned in cooperation with sympathetic Englishmen such as Octavian Hume) and like others of his generation who were part of the Bengali Renaissance, had been impressed by the liberal ideas of the English and believed in the benefits of an English education. He sent all his daughters and sons to school and university in England. The westernised Indian has been subject of a good deal of satire both in India and in England. Kipling had disliked this type of hybridity though it had been encouraged by an earlier breed of administrators. My Indian grandfather, who later became an alcoholic, had read Greats at Balliol (Grey's College and famous for taking so many Indians and Africans in the days when PC did not exist but a particular brand of liberalism did) and then studied Law and practised as a Barrister in Calcutta. He used to recite poetry to his children and via my mother I have a particular fondness for certain poems including Cory's translation of Heraclitus, which is the only poem I know in the original Greek.

> I wept as I remembered how often you and I
> Had tired the sun with talking and sent him down the sky
> And now that thou art lying, my dear old Carian guest,
> A handful of grey ashes long, long ago, at rest
> Still are they pleasant voices, thy nightingales awake
> For Death, he taketh all away, but them he cannot take.

Wystan's Professorship of Poetry coincided with my years at St Hugh's College, Oxford and I went to his lectures, later published in *The Dyer's Hand*, a proud niece thriving in reflected glory, delighted by the huge crowd which packed these occasions. I stayed a fourth year as I had started a B.Litt thesis on Shelley's Prose. Shelley's letters puzzled me for they could be cold but I was intrigued by the theatrical psychological scenarios of the Gothic novels I started researching in relation to the two he had written. I also felt infected by a sense of melancholy and stranded as though life was going on elsewhere – most of my friends having left. I abandoned the thesis and went to Florence to stay with Thekla and John Clark and Thekla's daughter Lisa, friends of Wystan and Chester Kallman. Unfortunately I caught meningitis in an epidemic and on Good Friday was taken by what, in my fevered imagination, were bandits (in reality volunteers incognito in surgical type masks on ambulance duty over Easter), to a hospital in Carregi, a large medical complex on the outskirts of Florence, where I spent a month under the care of Professor Vanucchi. I returned to London feeling I had gone through a sea change. During a slow process of recovery I tried, as I had done on and off through my life, to write, though always with an inhibitory awareness of Wystan and a fear of making a fool of myself.

William and I knew each other at Oxford. He was at New College. We used to go to films by Jean Cocteau and Ingmar Bergman: *La Belle et La Bête, Orphée, The Seventh Seal* and other sunnier Bergman films. We talked about literature and about Ezra Pound with whom William had started corresponding after reading *Rock-Drill* and reviewing it in *The Trifler* (the Westminster School literary magazine). He and his mother Rachel stayed with Pound when he left St Elizabeth's Hospital in America and moved to Rapallo in Northern Italy. Rita, my sister, and I also had an Italian connection for we had visited our Uncle Wystan in Ischia, far down in the south and reached him by taking a boat from Pozzuoli near Naples. We first stayed on our way from India to school in England.

While I worked on *Agenda*, it became obvious to me that William's loyalty to his 'house' poets was balanced by his Poundian concern with the historical engines of 'kulture' which drew on international voices. It came as a pleasant surprise when Eleni Cubitt, whom my family first met when my father worked in the Sudan, rang *Agenda* for some help with a programme which she and Dr Jenny Richardson, Director of The Foundation for Hellenic Culture were preparing. The idea was to pair 20th century Greek with English poets: Cavafy, Gatsos, Seferis, Ritsos and Elitis with Auden, MacNeice, Eliot, Dylan Thomas and, breaking the 20th century pairing, William Blake. Eleni had met Louis MacNeice when he stayed briefly with my parents in the Sudan. For the Cavafy/Auden double bill in September 1995, the speakers included David Ricks (on Cavafy) and Richard Davenport-Hines who had just published a biography of Auden.

If William was influenced by Pound, I was influenced by my uncle, though, of course, we were both influenced by other people too, not least our mothers. I found myself resistant to some of Pound's poetry, partly because of a dictatorship of opinion (both in Pound and in his admirers) which ran counter to my instincts. Wystan could of course sound and be dogmatic but differently. Poets can attract an admiring clique who seem to take over so that a personal appreciation becomes difficult but it is important to establish your own understanding of a poet, regardless of cliques, in an age when poets cannot rely on a community who share an idiom except sometimes in the limited world of academia. I was pleased that Dachine Rainer who died several years ago (her poetry was published in *Agenda*) liked both Pound and my uncle as people as well as admiring their poetry. She also liked the poetry of Ford Madox Ford and greatly admired e.e cummings. Dachine who was Jewish felt strongly that Pound had not been fairly dealt with and was highly critical of the lobby that was thwarting plans to put up a plaque in St. John the Divine. The problem of Pound and politics which has vexed so many is one that I had hoped to discuss with her and she could have been an important voice at the conference on Modern Poetry and Prejudice. On the question of prejudice and forgiveness I would like to quote from a poem published in *Agenda*, written by Norman Buller after visiting Wystan's grave in Kirchstetten with his wife, which uses lines from a number of Wystan's poems to create a meditation:

> As I, one of the many lives
> You never perceived, stand aware
> Of you this May morning, beneath
> Their stolid headstones and the arabesqued
> Ironwork of your Martyr's cross,
> The Kirchstetten dead, even the Nazi
> Suicide long-levelled in his
> Separate garden, are imperceptibly
> Crumbling back into their village
> As earth to earth.

The Nazi is the writer Josef Weinheber who would have been a neighbour of Chester's and Wystan's, had he not killed himself, and Wystan addressed him as a neighbour in the full Christian sense of the term in his poem 'Josef Weinheber'.

Just as William felt that he had to defend Pound against a particular climate of opinion I began to feel that I had to defend Wystan against a good deal of wrong comment and that I was in some curious tug-of-war where I was pulling for him and a different approach to poetry while William (and others) seemed too sure of the meaning of greatness or for that matter too sure about poetry. I found myself reacting against all of this and yearning for lines with simple mnemonic qualities, no claims to greatness, and with their own peculiar integrity of idiom (even cliché) whether light or serious or odd – a recognition of the human value of 'Those good foolish songs of ours' of which Primo Levi speaks.

*The above contains adapted extracts from a longer piece: Remembering William and Agenda, which is now on the Agenda website **www.agendapoetry.co.uk** in the History of Agenda section.*

Dylan Willoughby

Dusk at St. Marks, As Seen From Dunkin Donuts

The spire silhouettes a fire
The dark stamen of a flame
Its anther fringed by whorls
Of browning oranges
Isn't this happening enough?
I ask myself and slurp
My coffee.

This is my salon
Des refuses, no-one's refused.
Its windows offer cheaper views.
Saying the words is the
Prayer, a homeless man
Preaches. The prayer is
The saying. He's burnished
By dusk too. The words
And the light are his home,
He says, but we all know
That's not right.

                 Outside
They're wrapping up a TV
Shoot, leaving fake snow
And ice before the church.
People trudge and laugh at
This summer blizzard, snowball
Fights erupt before the quick thaw.
I think of Avedon's shot of Auden,
Peering through the squall, hands
Tucked into his overcoat, looking
At us – here – as the dusk does its burying

Note: Written in Auden's old neighborhood in New York's East Village, where Dylan Willoughby too lived for several years.

Patricia McCarthy

The Long Hurt of it

For W.H. Auden and Chester Kallman

It had no name.
The Yiddisher momma impersonations
he performed for you in bed
dressed you in her pleated skin

while he buried in your lap his head.
No cat's cradles, no left or right hand
for this crooked straightening game.

It had no name.
As you shadow-boxed the wedded lover
you had been for his crevices and folds –
to the slopes of his heart, under cover,

you put yourself on hold:
Eros losing to Agape. Your willing body
stuck with a has-been predator's shame.

It had no name.
You invented charm after charm
for jealousy, and from the hollows
inside his bones, sighted his arms

round callboys in winking windows.
Incest with him as Oedipus might have
cancelled pimps from the frame.

It had no name.
He was your marble David in Florence,
your Discobolus Thrower from Greece.
But you lay with him, a pietà, too intense

to requisition long-term release
from paterfamilias and flying tricksters
dancing in drag with inner dames.

It had no name.
Brünnhilde encircled him with fire.
Keenings haunted the wind.
He was your redeemer, healer, Messiah.

Yet to your lame shadow you were pinned.
Beside him, you dreamt he was your lover;
woke to no touch for momma, self-blame.

The long hurt of it simply had no name.

Rüdiger Görner

From Iceland to Kirchstetten

On W.H. Auden's verbal Journeys

i

Poetry introduces words at work; for the words of poetry do not rest in a verse; they rhyme or alliterate; they form, like musical compositions, dissonances or resonate harmoniously; and they are in constant motion transforming themselves in the eyes of the reader, changing colour and profile. Words travel through time and work towards some vague or specific meaning against the backdrop of the unknown. The way we read them is like the light and shade cast on a landscape; except that in the case of poetry we should rather speak of wordscapes through which the reader moves lured and led by the words' and poet's traces.

Take any opening of a poem. It establishes verbal correspondences indicating the beginning of a small new world; symbolically, they refer us back to the origins of thought and expression. The same could be said for certain opening chords of a musical piece that linger on for numerous bars, say, in E-flat or an indeterminable key. Artistic expression functions in terms of establishing correlations, in W.H. Auden's case between the word and conceptions of restlessness, utmost verbal concentration or rather, poignancy of expression, and the voyaging of images, to use Joyce's expression.

With all this said, we have already entered W.H. Auden's rather puzzling poetic world which was, and wanted to be, a world of its own, even though at no stage unrelated to the worlds of different realities that surrounded and conditioned it. Auden wrote with the ear of a musician; and his sense of poetic structure was informed by a painter's eye. He came across as a transatlantic European with an Oxford accent, at home in the bars of New York, familiar with hot springs on Iceland and Ischia, the College high table and the emphatic rurality of Lower Austria.

To celebrate this author means to celebrate one of the most relentless celebrators of language who indulged in 'light verse' as much as he explored faith-inspired profundity. There is the deeply humane poet, the lonely lover, anxious to protect his solitude and, at the same time, desperate for human warmth; there is the snob who refused an invitation to the White House on grounds of Harry S. Truman's being so 'thoroughly lower middle class', a poet with the appearance of a man of fashion photographed by Cecil Beaton but, in later years, that of a down and out. 'Intellectual disgrace/Stares from every human face'; perhaps this was also directed against his critics of whom he had many, particularly after his decision not to return from the United States to Britain during the war. Was it true that one of the most English of British poets was genuinely unpatriotic? This somewhat pathetic question raised at the time by Evelyn Waugh and others may have provided some of the subtext that caused the rather low-key Auden-celebrations in the past centenary year. In October 2006 the BBC admitted that they had so far forgotten to commission a programme on Auden. All attention was on John Betjeman's centenary to whom, incidentally, Auden had dedicated his poetic composition *The Age of Anxiety*. Had it not been for the intervention of Andrew Motion and Peter Porter, official Britain may still have ignored Auden's centenary altogether. Serious Auden scholarship realized in time that the œuvre of this poet cannot only be explained in the context of queer studies. The melancholic gaiety of this gay poet, his verbal and thematic virtuosity and the complexities of his attitude to ideology and religious belief were such that any form of 'single cause explanations' would only lead to intellectual sclerosis. Small wonder that the most challenging contribution of scholars to the Auden centenary was not yet another investigation into the nature and poetic representation of his gayness but a study on his unorthodox views on Christianity (by Arthur Kirsch, Yale 2007).

Now then, meet Auden, the restless globe-trotter. It might be an idea to erect an Auden-statue in one of the terminals at Heathrow once they have been brought up to the level of St. Pancras where Betjeman is now residing in eloquent monumental silence. There he was, Auden, the world citizen, who was at home in California and Kirchstetten, this staggeringly undiplomatic ambassador of the republic of poets. Meet Auden, the advocate of authenticity in a world of simulation; a genuine wit and melancholic whose partner for some significant time was, according to those who knew them, the campest of all, his-co-librettist and lover Chester Kallman; meet Auden, the sting in our world of political correctness and the provider of unforgettable poetic moments, most prominently so when John Hannah playing the part of Matthew recites 'Stop all the clocks', Auden's 'Funeral Blues', in Mike Newell's film *Four Weddings and a Funeral*; Auden's omnipresence was confirmed when New Yorkers, in the aftermath of the terrorist attacks on September eleventh, somewhat misleadingly, decided to adopt his poem 'September 1, 1939' as their mourning song.

'For we are conscripts to our age/Simply by being born; we wage/The war we are.' There is something terrifying in Auden's simplicity of expression, or rather phrasing of thoughts and images. His choreography of words (for he made words dance before the eyes of the reader) can amount to amusing and haunting verbal scenes. This was a poet of table talks who took delight in asking absurd questions or making statements of the following kind: 'Wagner's Brünnhilde is as old as God and much heavier'. Or: 'Has English acting declined since Henry Irving?'

Auden writing libretti for Stravinsky ('The Rake's Progress') and Henze ('Elegy for Young Lovers') and other texts for William Walton and Pablo Casals, always wanted to fuse grand opera with high mass, as Christopher Isherwood once remarked, if only the composers had allowed him to do that. He was the composer's poet; for he wrote like a musician, as Benjamin Britten was quick to realize. But the very poetic form in which Auden excelled was the elegy, for instance his elegies for Yeats and Freud, not to speak of his grand scale elegy in prose 'The Age of Anxiety' or the prose-poem 'The Sea and the Mirror'. Beaton, incidentally, liked to photograph him against the backdrop of mirrors which would catch his profile. As in Coleridge's poetry, Auden's poetic personae undertake journeys to the heart of loss. Their soul can be spelt like 'sole', too, indicating the intricate connection between spirituality and solitude. The best of Auden's poetry is informed by his idiosyncratic expression of religious faith. In later years he made a point of quoting Lichtenberg's aphorism: 'There is a great difference between *still* believing something and believing it *again*.' Auden was the very one who believed his beliefs again and again but therefore always anew. With James of the New Testament Auden could have said: 'Faith if it does not lead to action is in itself a lifeless thing.' Action of that sort consisted in Auden's case of happily agreeing to marry Erika Mann in June 1935 in order to provide her with British citizenship after her expulsion from Germany. Klaus Mann had approached him with this 'urgent family request' after Christopher Isherwood rejected the proposal on grounds that his mother would disapprove of such practices. Auden's brother-in-law, Golo Mann, remembers him as a poet who wavered between ultra-modernism and Alexander Pope and followed William James's principle of the 'will to believe'. Already then was Auden capable of mimicking the hyper-modernist who dissolved rhythm and coherence and of being the parodist of Tennyson capable of writing verses like these (on Yeats's death in 1939): 'Follow, poet, follow right/To the bottom of the night …/In the deserts of the heart/Let the healing fountain start.' In those 'deserts of the heart' Auden was looking for an oasis for the soul. He looked for it in Iceland in a failed attempt to escape fascist Europe, at St. Mark's Place, New York, and in Austria, the country of Hofmannsthal whom he admired for having written masterly libretti that could be read without music.

ii

Auden and Austria is more than an alliteration. It is the name for a poetic synergy. Auden, the New Yorker from York, graduate from Oxford with a third class degree in English, settled in a place that some would call cosy, others forsaken – a mere hamlet with some thirteen hundred inhabitants in the county of Sankt Pölten, quintessentially rural and arch-conservative, the anti-New York, if ever there was one. As far as one can tell, Auden, the cosmopolitan, cherished every moment in this place. Golo Mann remembered visiting Auden in Kirchstetten in 1963 where he also met his housekeepers, Emma Eiermann, and her brother, Josef, German refugees from former Bohemia. After 1945 both had been expelled from Czechoslovakia under cruel circumstances; to Auden they epitomized victims of power politics. Auden, by instinct, took sides with them to the point that, on his housekeeper's death, he wrote a heart-rendering elegy in her memory, which is however not devoid in bizarre Audenesque logic: 'Liebe Frau Emma,/na, was hast Du denn gemacht?/You who always made/such conscience of our comfort,/oh, how could you go and die,// as if you didn't know/that in a permissive age/so rife with envy,/a housekeeper is harder to replace than a lover'.

Kirchstetten touched and bemused him, Austria concerned him. It was his idyll and his haven; it was his solace and his retreat. In his elegy 'Whitsunday in Kirchstetten' of July 1962 he comprehensively described his impressions connected with this place, including the Lower-Austrian accent and his own meandering associations: '... when just now/Kirchstetten prayed for the dead, only I/remembered Franz Joseph the Unfortunate, who danced/once in eighty-six years and never/used the telephone'. But literally 'above all' Auden reflects a sentiment of real concern: 'In the onion-tower overhead/bells clash at the Elevation, calling/ on Austria to change'. The elegy is not short of shrewd social and political asides either: 'no doubt, if the Allies had not/conquered the Ost-Mark, if the dollar fell,/ the *Gemütlichkeit* would be less ...'

What Auden observed was still a very different Austria from the country it is today, always in danger of being marginalized, if not shipwrecked in the backwaters of Western Europe for good, as she was for most parts uncomfortably surrounded by the iron curtain. 'What has poor Austria done/to draw such disapproval?/ The *Beamterei*, it's true,/is as awful as ever,/the drivers are dangerous,/standards at the Staatsoper/steadily decline each year,/and *Wien*'s become provincial/compared to the pride She was./Still, it's a cosy country,/unracked by riots or strikes/and backward at drug-taking...'

But there was more to his image of Austria than Kirchstetten and Viennese *Schmäh* on the state of culture. This became apparent in an elegy on Josef Weinheber which he wrote twenty years after the poet's suicide. In this elegy, Auden was one of the first to remember Franz Jägerstätter of St Radegund 'who said his lonely/ Nein to the Aryan State/and was beheaded'. One year before, the publication of Auden's Weinheber elegy Jägerstätter, whose case has recently received renewed attention following his beatification through the Pope, had been the subject of a study by Gordon C. Zahn (*In Solitary Witness*). This inspired the peace movement in America and prompted Daniel Ellsberg to spearhead the anti-Vietnam protests. (It is worth noting, too, that Axel Corti, who knew Auden, produced in 1971 a film called 'Der Fall Jägerstätter' with Kurt Weinzierl in the title role.)

The elegy on Weinheber is neither an attempt on Auden's part to blame nor to exonerate this ingenious but politically corrupted poet who took his life because he could no longer come to terms with his temporary involvement in the culture of brown-shirt barbarity. In more than one way Weinheber existed between 'gods and demons', to quote his poetic composition of 1938 and it is there where Auden in his poem located him. Moreover, Auden sensed an uncomfortably elective affinity with this poet turned alcoholic, a fellow-Kirchstettener, who had allowed himself to be taken in by ideology. 'Categorised enemies/twenty years ago,/now next-door neighbors, we might/have become good friends,/sharing a common ambit/and love of the Word,/over a golden *Kremser*/had many a long/langue on syntax, commas,/versification.'

What cannot be verified can at least be versified. Auden realized that he now shared the same views of the landscape that once Weinheber had ('Looking across our valley'), namely onto the now 'impaled green,/committed thereafter den/*Abgrund zu nennen*.' (The latter being an indirect invocation of Hölderlin's

40

fragment 'Vom Abgrund nämlich haben/ Wir angefangen [...]') German, or so it seems, is the ever present neighbouring language, as it were, in Auden's poetry. It is as if he used references to German, be it from Novalis or Karl Kraus (for example his maxim, 'Die Sprache ist die Mutter, nicht die Magd, des Gedankens': Language is the mother, not the maid of thought) to authenticate the philosophical ambition of his poetry.

But Auden and Austria was by no means a one-sided affair. When I was asked to compile an anthology of Auden's love poetry with German translations I found, perhaps to my surprise, Austrian poets in the forefront of Auden-translators, among them Ernst Jandl, Erich Fried and Hilde Spiel. Moreover, it was Ingeborg Bachmann who had taken Auden's *The Age of Anxiety* to heart. Recent research (Christine Kanz) has found compelling evidence for the intricate connection between Auden's poetic composition on an existential condition and Bachmann's novel *Malina* and her *Todesarten*-project to the point that 'Malina' is the feminised version of Auden's Malin, besides Quant, Rosetta and Emble the fourth protagonist in his 'baroque eclogue'. Auden's Malin, a member of the Canadian Air Force, analyses the barbarian in us who is bred in factories and 'corporate companies'; 'college towns/Mothered his mind, and many journals/Backed his beliefs'. Malin fears that common sense might be privatised and, in so doing, man would establish the worst possible type of individualism. Bachmann's Malina is many things but camouflaged as an employee at the Austrian Military Museum whilst all anxieties are bundled in the narrator's *Ich*. This *Ich* is afraid of human relationships breaking up and people drifting apart. Auden's quartet of protagonists finds itself reduced to a trio in Bachmann's novel (Ivan, Malina, Ich); together they would form a septet and it would indeed be tempting to make Auden's Malin meet Bachmann's Malina, his Rosetta falling love with her Ivan, Emble pairing up with Bachmann's Ich, and Auden's Quant rekindling anxieties in all three couples, splitting them up and joining them together in new configurations.

iii

Auden argued that it is in verse not prose that the logic of an argument is most radically exposed. He even felt that verse could make 'ideas too clear and distinct', more Cartesian in other words. Well, in his 'last will and testament' which concludes the *Letters from Iceland*, Auden and his friend and travel companion Louis MacNeice leave to 'Wittgenstein who writes such hits/As the Tractatus Logico-Philosophicus/all readers who can spare the wits.' What they had hoped for on Iceland was remoteness and distance from the political madness in Europe only to find that the Icelanders were only too happy to welcome KdF travellers (Kraft Durch Freude, the Nazi tourist organisation, mainly for workers, enabling them to travel to foreign places for the first time) from Germany who were in search of Germanic purity in the North: 'Down in Europe Seville fell,/Nations germinating hell,/The Olympic games were run -/Spots upon the Aryan sun.' The truth of poems must be self-evident, Auden once remarked; to be precise he said

41

this in his 'unwritten poem' which he called with Goethe *Dichtung und Wahrheit*, a pseudo-autobiographical text that is about the impossibility of writing a plausible autobiography. Linguistic playfulness and the quest for poetic truth were the two sides of Auden's word-coins; for language was to him a currency subject to inflation and devaluation as much as to deflation. He knew what he and his words were worth. Part of his art was to find a rhyme even then when the discrepancies between two positions he depicted were irreconcilable or distinctly non-sensical, positions of the following kind: 'Let us be cheery/like English Bishops/on the Quantum Theory' or as in his collection of *Academic Graffiti*: 'Joseph Haydn/ Never read Dryden/Nor did John Dryden/Ever hear Haydn.'

The truth of Auden's poetry was a truth in the poetic making. As Stephen Spender once remarked, Auden's poems were written, as it were, on his much commented face with its weather and life-beaten features and its skin in later years wrinkled to the point of furrowed. His facial lines resembled grooves, even a landscape perhaps.

After Auden's funeral Spender wrote in a poem of the same title: 'The white October sun circles Kirchstetten/With colours of chrysanthemums in gardens,/ And bronze and golden under wiry boughs,/A few last apples gleam like jewels./ Back in the village inn, we sit on benches/For the last toast to you, the honoured ghost/Whose absence now becomes incarnate in us.' In its conclusion the poem speaks of Auden's poems as 'paradigms of love' which were drawn back into the circle 'of your unfolding solitude'. Love indeed; for Auden's poetry is but a manifestation of love, a long series of variations on the theme 'Io t'amo', that wanted to be ceaseless. In *Dichtung und Wahrheit* though, which circles around the meaning of love in poetry, Auden exposed this most universal of sentiments to a particular test of time with unmatched irony: '"I will love You forever," swears the poet. I find this easy to swear, too. *I will love You at 4:15 p.m. next Tuesday*; is that still as easy?' Autobiography is auto-invention and projection, as Auden's 'unwritten poem' testifies, or as he writes about 'Paul Valéry/Earned a meagre salary,/Walking through the *Bois*,/Observing his *Moi*.' Not to speak of 'Alexander Pope/ [who] Never gave up hope/Of finding a motto/To affix to his Grotto.' The simplicity of Auden's verse often veils uncanny complexities: 'A sentence uttered makes a world appear/Where all things happen as it says they do;/We doubt the speaker, not the tongue we hear:/Words have no word for words that are not true.' Often, Auden's poems sound like a hybrid of shortened limericks and riddles; occasionally, they turn a scholarly endeavour into sublime parody as with his poetic 'commentary on Shakespeare's *The Tempest*', which turned out to be a highly original transformation of critical thought and poetic transfiguration, composed under the title *The Sea and the Mirror* (1942/44).

The memorial stone for Auden at Poets' Corner in Westminster Abbey bears his verse: 'In the prison of his days/Teach the free man how to praise'. The praising of life against literally all the odds of existence and history, once Rilke's great theme, was re-introduced by Auden into the poetic discourse. The question of whether we as critically minded people can afford to be affirmative in the days of negative dialectics concerned him more than others. Nowhere can we find this problem more illuminatingly, and controversially, expressed than in the final stanza of his poem 1ˢᵗ September 1939: 'Defenceless under the night/Our world in stupor lies;/ Yet, dotted everywhere,/Ironic points of light/Flash out wherever the Just/Exchange their messages:/May I, composed like them/Of Eros and of dust,/Beleaguered by the same/Negation and despair,/Show an affirming flame.'

This question without question marks is of Nietzschean origin. But on Nietzsche directly Auden only had to say: 'Nietzsche/Had the habit as a teacher/Of cracking his joints/To emphasize his points.' Thus joked W.H. Auden, the cosmopolitan bard, buried in Kirchstetten.

John Greening

Bird Lore

Through that forest of dead words
I would hunt the living birds
                    Louis MacNeice, 'Postscript to Iceland'

Golden Plover

Beautiful, certainly, in its braided
shawl and cap, but William Morris
insisted it be useful too
so he shot a pair for supper:
the taste was questionable.

Arctic Tern

The terns that divebomb you
down by the Tjörn are only
defending their precious vowels
with low-flying shrieks
against another Occupation.

Oystercatcher

Nuns concealing their flash
of pyritic lipstick
praying on the edge of the
great pagan sea and hammering
psalms to the thunderer.

Whimbrel

What warbling at the Althing
from the booth of seven whistlers –
no Lawspeaker could learn it
or recite this ululation
of outlaws in the wilderness.

Steven O'Brien

Scrying Stone

for Louis MacNeice on Achill

A green tooth
Of the hound of the sea
Lies pendant in my hand.

My thumb is a strop,
Fetching up shine
From its mackerel bands.
Its undercurrent
Is fish-slip
And mint gleam.

I see you last Easter
Gleaning
For this true marble,
Littering the Achill shallows.

Its edge,
The nip and brine
Of a mermaid's bite.

Its back,
A sealed locket
Of her jade hair.

Its face,
A storm-cast watch,
Set ticking
The instant you clutched it
In cold fingers.

By your first gift -
This scrying stone
Notched, plumb and gainly
I will know you.

Peter McDonald

'This mirror of wet sand':
Louis MacNeice's Achill Poems

In the early pages of his first post-war collection of poems, *Holes in the Sky* (1948), Louis MacNeice placed the short piece, 'Corner Seat':[1]

> Suspended in the moving night
> The image in the next-door train
> Looks at first sight as self-assured
> As you do, traveller. Look again:
>
> Windows between you and the world
> Keep out the cold, keep out the fright;
> Then why does your reflection seem
> So lonely in the moving night?

There is a density to this – a packing-in of the turns of thought and meaning – which suggests the epigrammatic; and the direct address to 'you', the 'traveller', sounds a deliberate echo of the classical *siste viator* ['traveller, pause']. But the poem isn't quite an epigram, or rather it is an epigram which has been allowed to go wrong, for the lines fail to deliver any clinching certainties. Instead, the poem works towards a question without an answer, about a 'you' who, far from pausing, is carried through a 'moving night', reduplicated in a reflection and yet not 'self-assured' but 'lonely', or seeming so. The visual, which in much of MacNeice's poetry (and especially in this writing of the 1930s) is so strong an element as almost to constitute a driving force, is becoming here something self-complicating and self-perplexing. And the proximity of the addressed 'you' to the voice of many MacNeice poems – and, more directly, to the much-travelling MacNeice himself – adds another doubleness to this two-stanza poem about one thing looking at another: a poem written by MacNeice speaks to MacNeice about another pairing, 'you and the world', which appears to have been blocked by self-assurance. Glass protects against the night, but can also reflect in the night: the carriage windows make that self-assurance possible, as they 'Keep out the cold, keep out the fright', but they also make possible the show of reflections between the two trains, in which the 'self-assured' perceives itself as 'lonely'.

The tensions between impulses here are familiar ones in MacNeice's writing,

---

[1] Louis MacNeice, *Collected Poems* ed. Peter McDonald (London: Faber and Faber, 2007), p. 805: this is the text as published in *Holes in the Sky*; for the later version, as revised by MacNeice for *Eighty-Five Poems* (1959), see *Collected Poems* p. 255.

and they can be paralleled in many poems both before and after *Holes in the Sky*. But the situation of 'Corner Seat', and of the volume in which it was collected, is one where such tensions have both historical specificity and resonance. How MacNeice sees himself is, certainly, the kind of issue that can all too easily become indistinct, covered in the fluff of generalisation and truism; critically, it might be one of those common (but still futile) grounds on which to exercise one's gifts for critical platitude. Yet 'Corner Seat' is a poem which concentrates this problem of seeing oneself as something productive and provocative; what it produces, and what it provokes, come within a context of MacNeice's wariness and caution in seeing himself as this or that and – more specifically – his ability (or otherwise) and his willingness (or otherwise) to see himself as he was sometimes seen, as Irish. In *Holes in the Sky*, this means MacNeice seeing himself in Ireland, for at the centre of the book there is a series of poems written in and about Ireland, which were the fruits of MacNeice's post-war 'sabbatical' in the West in 1945.

If MacNeice's War had been a busily creative one, it had also been creatively exhausting, and the frantic pace of MacNeice's BBC work, as a writer and producer (often at short notice) of everything from elaborate epic drama to literary and topographical features, all to a greater or lesser extent under the umbrella of Britain's propaganda effort, had taken its toll. The period of leave which took MacNeice (and his family) to Achill in 1945 was justified to his employers as one in which much new work could be conceived and have its gestation. This was, indeed, a promise on which MacNeice made good, for his best radio drama, *The Dark Tower*, began to take shape in this period. Unofficially, MacNeice spoke of the trip to Ireland as a consequence of his 'allergy to England'.[2] The poems written during this stay show signs of the allergy, as well as bringing with them the legacy of MacNeice's already complicated feelings about Ireland itself.

One, relatively recent, aspect of that complication lay in the War that had just ended. MacNeice's attitudes to Ireland at the beginning and by the end of the War were probably different, and certainly issued in different literary expressions: this can be gauged by comparing the sequence 'The Coming of War' in *Plant and Phantom* (1941) with the short, laconically (and ironically) Yeatsian lyric 'Neutrality' in *Springboard* (1944). 'Corner Seat' is very much a post-war poem, placed as it is after the air-raid song 'The Streets of Laredo' and the poem 'Hiatus', about the War in England as 'The years that did not count', to be followed by the poem 'Aftermath', where 'the bandaging dark which bound/ This town together is loosed'.[3] These are not poems of victory, but of anticlimax and disillusion. The poems from MacNeice's Irish 'sabbatical' are not post-war in this sense, but they are (more problematically) post-Emergency. Here, matters of disillusion take on a slightly different cast, and the sense of anticlimax is something located more in

---

[2] See Barbara Coulton, *Louis MacNeice in the BBC* (London: Faber and Faber, 1980), p. 78.
[3] Louis MacNeice, *Collected Poems* pp. 254-5.

MacNeice himself than in the place he visits.

One question in these Irish poems, then, is that of how MacNeice sees himself. The whole matter is raised at length in a poem from the period that stands slightly to one side of the poems from the West – or rather slightly to the north of them – 'Carrick Revisited'. The author of the earlier 'Carrickfergus' returns changed to this childhood home, and the principal difference is that panorama has been replaced by introspection. The town of MacNeice's first poem (which appeared in *The Earth Compels* (1937)) was remembered during the First World War; in this 1945 sequel, the poem's first question is 'Which war was which?', and MacNeice moves quickly to give an account of the complications of memory and place:[4]

> Who was – and am – dumbfounded to find myself
> In a topographical frame – here, not there –
> The channels of my dreams determined largely
> By random chemistry of soil and air;
> Memories I had shelved peer at me from the shelf.

The voice here does not look back on memories; the memories 'peer at' him, back on display in his 'topographical frame'. The condition of being 'here, not there' gives 'Carrick Revisited' a charge of unfamiliarity in its account of a return to familiar places; and the self being contemplated by its own memories is doubly framed – by a remembered childhood and by an even earlier context, that of deeper family history:

> Torn before birth from where my fathers dwelt,
> Schooled from the age of ten to a foreign voice,
> Yet neither western Ireland nor southern England
> Cancels this interlude; what chance misspelt
> May never now be righted by my choice.
>
> Whatever then my inherited or acquired
> Affinities, such remains my childhood's frame
> Like a belated rock in the red Antrim clay
> That cannot at this era change its pitch or name –
> And the pre-natal mountain is far away.

In a short piece on her childhood in Carrickfergus, MacNeice's sister Elizabeth Nicholson remembered that 'We were in our minds a West of Ireland family exiled from our homeland.'[5] Both paternal and maternal lines did, in fact, go back into the

---

[4] Ibid., pp. 261-2.

[5] Elizabeth Nicholson, 'Trees Were Green', in Terence Brown and Alec Reid (eds.), *Time Was Away: The World of Louis MacNeice* (Dublin: Dolmen Press, 1974, p.14.)

West and, if Connemara was often spoken of in the MacNeice family with a degree of nostalgia, then this was for the children, as the poet remembered, 'nostalgia for somewhere I had never been'.[6] 'Carrick Revisited' might seem to verge on the melodramatic when it speaks of being 'Torn before birth from where my fathers dwelt' – and there is nothing in the poem itself to temper this impression – but MacNeice is probably in earnest: his father had indeed, early on, been driven off the island of Omey in a sectarian dispute. MacNeice finds two images for the 'here' and 'there' of Carrick and Connemara, the 'belated rock in the red Antrim clay' and 'the pre-natal mountain'. It is hard to see how an unmoving rock can have 'pitch', but this 'pitch' that it cannot change returns the image to the 'foreign voice' to which the speaker has been 'schooled'. 'Belated' stands in apposition to 'pre-natal', as both rock and mountain, the too late and the too early, themselves frame the 'childhood's frame', reapproached in what MacNeice calls 'this interlude'.

Stone of any kind is seldom what one might identify as a strongly positive element in MacNeice's imagery: from early work onwards, it has connotations of stasis, paralysis, and worse. The mountain and the rock are not, therefore, promising symbols when they stand to either side of the writing voice. In another, much weaker, poem from this period, MacNeice presents a pair of lovers as a fact that 'Cannot be generalized away' (though why one would want to try this, aside perhaps from their being named, gratingly, 'Tom and Tessy', MacNeice does not explain). These lovers are very much 'here, not there':[7]

> Tom is here, Tessy is here
> At this point in a given year
> With all this hour's accessories,
> A given glory – and to look
> That gift-horse in the mouth will prove
> Or disprove nothing of their love
> Which is as sure intact a fact,
> Though young and supple, as what stands
> Obtuse and old, in time congealed,
> Behind them as they mingle hands –
> Self-contained, unexplained,
> The cromlech in the clover field.

This is verbose, of course, and a good example of how MacNeice's facility for verse can sometimes work in unfortunate conjunction with his ability to produce a wordy eloquence that does little more than mark time. Nevertheless, these lovers whose life is overlooked, but not reduced in either value or agency by the prehistoric stone monument are symbols of an independence for which MacNeice

---

[6] Louis MacNeice, *The Strings Are False: An Unfinished Autobiography* (London: Faber and Faber, 1965), p. 217.

[7] Louis MacNeice, *Collected Poems*, p. 261.

himself evidently hoped (and which, in an artistic sense, he wanted the break from the work of London to provide). There could, in fact, be autobiographical content lurking beneath 'Tom and Tessy', for MacNeice and his fiancée Mary had visited Achill in 1929, and seen (or, as the poem might have it, had been seen by) the megalithic tombs and cromlechs on the slopes of Slievemore. This cromlech, 'obtuse and old' as it is, remains 'Self-contained, unexplained', as though its self-sufficiency still marks a threat. Like the 'belated rock' and the 'pre-natal mountain', the cromlech is part of a landscape (and an Irish landscape) which both threatens individuality and also underwrites it. A version of the image had ended MacNeice's 'The conscript' in *Springboard* (1944), as 'That dignity which far above him burns/ In stars that yet are his and which below/ Stands rooted like a dolmen in his spine.'[8]

'Western Landscape' is another poem in this sequence where MacNeice's habits of verbal elaboration and rhetorical effect, developed especially in his wartime broadcasting work, inflate a poem to something bigger than its right size. The versification and the length between them make 'Western Landscape' an over-excited and over-loud performance (much talk of St Brandan the Navigator, along with some uncharacteristically bleary-eyed mysticism about the desire to 'undo/ Time in quintessential West'), but it helps to provide the co-ordinates for MacNeice's 'interlude'. 'The west of Ireland,' MacNeice writes, 'Is brute and ghost at once'; this simultaneous concreteness and impalpability is something which the visitor – or rather this particular visitor – feels 'in passing/ Among these shadows of this permanent show'. Again, the permanence which stares down the speaker's own impermanence is a stony one. The poem's closing crescendo is built around the plea to 'Let me ... Here add one stone to the indifferent cairn':[9]

> Let me at least in token that my mother
> Earth was a rocky earth with breasts uncovered
> To suckle solitary intellects
> And limber instincts, let me, if a bastard
> Out of the West by urban civilization
> (Which unwished father claims me – so I must take
> What I can before I go) let me who am neither Brandan
> Free of all roots nor yet a rooted peasant
> Here add one stone to the indifferent cairn ...
> With a stone on the cairn, with a word on the wind, with a prayer
>   in the flesh let me honour this country.

'My mother/ Earth': seldom can have an enjambment have done so much work so unconvincingly, and it is probably a weakness in the poem that it is not possible

---

[8] Ibid., p. 225.
[9] Ibid., p. 267.

to be sure whether MacNeice is tripping himself up here or deliberately allowing the poetry to take a fall. Whatever may be the case, the poem puts squarely in the foreground an identification of the West with the maternal, and its opposite, the disappointingly flat 'urban civilization', with an 'unwished father'. All this can have biographical resonance, undoubtedly; but it also jars with much of MacNeice's sense of his own life, to such an extent that one has to wonder whether the poet's rhetoric is actually leading him into a kind of autobiographical gaffe, since both of the poet's parents had roots in the West of Ireland.

Two other 1945 poems, 'Last before America' and 'Littoral', project the west in terms of fractured family relations. For both, the sea is a surrounding or encroaching element; at times, it seems that it is the land that encroaches upon the sea. The first stanza of 'Littoral' presents a shoreline that simultaneously traces and erases the 'runes' it seems to make:[10]

> Indigo, mottle of purple and amber, ink,
> Damson whipped with cream, improbable colours of sea
> And unanalysable rhythms – fingering foam
> Tracing, erasing its runes, regardless
> Of you and me
> And whether we think it escape or the straight way home.

'Regardless' here answers the intensity of regard which the poem itself is paying to the sea's 'improbable colours'. That intensity soon runs up against the diminished returns of near-tautology, when 'The sand here looks like metal, there it feels like fur,/ The wind films the sand with sand', so that the poet's descriptive resources seem to be stuck, leaving unanalysed the sea that began the poem, now the 'Brain-bound or heart-bound sea – old woman or old man – / To whom we are ciphers, creatures to ignore.' Like the cromlech, the Atlantic here is still 'Self-contained, unexplained', but it is also humanized, albeit in a bleak way, as an old man or woman stuck somehow, whether in brain or heart. 'Last before America' sharpens the historical point of such intuitions, feeling in the landscape itself the loss of an emigrant population:[11]

> At night the accordion melts in the wind from the sea
> From the bourne of emigrant uncle and son, a defeated
> Music that yearns and abdicates; chimney-smoke and spindrift
> Mingle and part as ghosts do. The decree
> Of the sea's divorce is final.

---

[10] Ibid., p. 259.
[11] Ibid., p. 264.

This adds force to the poem's final image, of 'certain long low islets snouting towards the west/ Like cubs that have lost their mother'. Again, questions arise of MacNeice's own biographical investment in his imagery; but these are not questions that are very easily answered.

The most important of MacNeice's Achill poems of 1945 is certainly 'The Strand'. Here, autobiographical content is more definitely present, and is made explicit. The poem is, in part at least, an elegy for the poet's father, John Frederick MacNeice, who had died in 1942.[12]

> White Tintoretto clouds beneath my naked feet,
> This mirror of wet sand imputes a lasting mood
> To island truancies; my steps repeat
>
> Someone's who now has left such strands for good
> Carrying his boots and paddling like a child,
> A square black figure whom the horizon understood –
>
> My father. Who for all his responsibly compiled
> Account books of a devout, precise routine
> Kept something in him solitary and wild,
>
> So loved the western sea and no tree's green
> Fulfilled him like these contours of Slievemore
> Menaun and Croaghaun and the bogs between.
>
> Sixty-odd years behind him and twelve before,
> Eyeing the flange of steel in the turning belt of brine
> It was sixteen years ago he walked this shore
> And the mirror caught his shape which catches mine
> But then as now the floor-mop of the foam
> Blotted the bright reflections – and no sign
>
> Remains of face or feet when visitors have gone home.

Several elements from the other poems regroup here – the sea foam, for example, and the mountains of Achill – but the poem far exceeds all of its immediate neighbours in power and complexity. The slight flatness of 'Littoral''s 'The wind films the sand with sand' is improved upon by something less studied, but more productive, when MacNeice makes 'This mirror of wet sand' a central device. For what the speaker sees in this mirror is himself, but himself doubled: 'my steps repeat/Someone's' (and the

---

12 Ibid., pp. 263-4.

emjambment here sets up an altogether subtler suspense and postponement than Western Landscape's 'mother/ Earth'), with 'Someone's' turning out to be those of 'My father'. Yet the 'mirror' is more complicated than that, for it sees the landscape through the people it reflects: along with a 'shape' it catches the mountains and bogs of Achill, against which these human figures are transitory as well as interchangeable, as though this sea-and-sand mirror, like the sea in 'Littoral', found them 'ciphers, creatures to ignore'. In the wiping away of images in the poem's final lines, when 'then as now, the floor-mop of the foam/ Blotted the bright reflections', this 'mirror of wet sand' prepares itself, perhaps, for other figures and their reflections. The poem's last words, 'when visitors have gone home' seem to accept the transitoriness which the image conveys. The voice of the poem is 'here, not there'; but the poem closes by sending it 'home' – there, not here.

Set on Achill, 'The Strand''s 'island truancies' carry a degree of autobiographical accuracy: MacNeice was on Achill during his 'sabbatical', but had also visited it before – most notably when, in the company of his father and stepmother, he brought Mary Beazley, his fiancée to the island in 1929. Mary and Louis's son, Dan, was later brought to the seaside on family holidays of his own; not with his mother (who had left him and Louis in 1935, and lived subsequently in the USA), but with the Bishop. A MacNeice family photograph from the late 1930s shows Dan on the beach with his grandfather, the Bishop's trousers rolled up as they walk, hand in hand, through the waves. Although the photograph is not from Achill, for MacNeice the *memory* is – at least insofar as it gives rise to the Achill poem 'The Strand'. The figure 'Carrying his boots and paddling like a child' might also, plausibly, be paddling *with* a child – the poet's grandson, perhaps, or, in his own childhood, the poet himself. And Louis MacNeice's 1945 trip had on it his own young daughter, Corinna. At all events, the image in this mirror is solidly patriarchal – or indeed patriarchally solid: 'A square black figure whom the horizon understood – // My father'. The firm end to the poem's first sentence, where the identification of that figure vaults over a stanza-break, is an effect of settling and embedding important to the poem as a whole. Its full-stop (which might, in fact, as easily have been a comma) enforces a hard pause before the line itself has had time to get properly moving. In that pause, the reader is also given pause: for although the syntax is 'my steps repeat/ Someone's ... A figure ...// My father' (not – as a result partly of the dash after 'understood' – 'My father's'), there is just enough residual force from 'This mirror of wet sand' to allow the possibility, for a moment only, that the mirror shows 'My father'. Is the phrase 'My father', in other words, an explanation or an identification? The pause given, because of a pause taken in the poem, makes the half-emergence of such a question part of MacNeice's effect.

The lines that follow, and provide a short portrait of the Bishop, work out more fully the implications of being a figure 'whom the horizon understood'. Again, things are subtly but noticeably reversed here, for this turns around the obvious (if slightly banal) idea of being someone who understood the horizon:

Who for all his responsibly compiled
Account books of a devout, precise routine
Kept something in him solitary and wild,

So loved the western sea and no tree's green
Fulfilled him like these contours of Slievemore
Menaun and Croaghaun and the bogs between.

The 'square, black figure' is now more the embodiment, or the physical shape, of an account book, where the 'devout, precise routine' can have its being; the other thing, the 'something' 'solitary and wild', is the sea and the mountains – these particular, named, mountains of Achill – which do not just 'fulfil' the Bishop in a weakly metaphorical sense, but actually give him something like an inner shape. To be 'Fulfilled' 'like these contours' is also – beneath the surface of the sentence, so to speak – to be filled full *by* these same contours. MacNeice's recurring notion of the western landscape, that it contemplates indifferently the human figures who pass before it, is present here, perhaps along with the idea that the landscape has somehow entered the Bishop, that the poet's father, dead now, is a part of the landscape now surrounding the poet. Seeing himself in 'this mirror of wet sand', MacNeice sees his own father; at the same time, he is aware that he is being seen, both by Achill itself and (by extension) by the father who has died into the permanence of that place.

It is at this point that MacNeice becomes specific about time as well as place. Evidently, the poet has been keeping 'account books' of his own:

Sixty-odd years behind him and twelve before,
Eyeing the flange of steel in the turning belt of brine
It was sixteen years ago he walked this shore

'Sixteen years ago' was 1929, and the holiday in Achill when Louis was accompanied by his fiancée; much had happened in those sixteen years, and there is of course a great deal of autobiographical content (for MacNeice) packed in to the dates which these lines contain. But that content is not really contained in the poem, which instead gives its account of time passing, watching the Bishop as he watches the ocean. The waves are made metallic, and functional, with their flange and belt; and this solidity, which in part answers to the solidity of the 'square black figure', is set in contrast to the sea's other aspect, which does not make solid but dissolves the 'bright reflections' on the wet sand:

… the mirror caught his shape which catches mine
But then as now the floor-mop of the foam
Blotted the bright reflections – and no sign

Remains of face or feet when visitors have gone home.

The sea's 'foam' is an agent of erasure, though MacNeice's metaphor here remains in key with the practicality, even functionality, of the imagery of 'account books', 'routine', 'flange', and 'belt', as its 'floor-mop' takes away, or obscures, both footsteps and images of father and son. The poem's last enjambment – which carries 'no sign' across a stanza-break to the final, isolated line, and 'Remains' – does its own share of wiping-away, in a carefully paced movement. The statement is simple, and final, enough: 'no sign// Remains' – there is nothing here – nothing now of the Bishop in whose long-gone footsteps MacNeice has been walking, and nothing in future of the poet's own steps. Father and son are 'visitors' who have gone, and are going, 'home'. And mirrors, of course, do not keep the images they carry. At the same time, MacNeice's last line, which stretches to a slow alexandrine, places 'Remains' in a strong position; in its own visual isolation, the line allows for the ghostly presence of what it does not actually mean – that something 'Remains'.

'Visitors' is a loaded word, but MacNeice means something more here than a straightforward identification of his own family with some kind of outsider status in the West. On the contrary, the poet (and this poem) are aware of family origins in the West of Ireland. 'Torn before birth from where my fathers dwelt', MacNeice himself understood that contingencies, of one kind and another, had given him a Northern Irish, rather than (say) a Connemara background. But some of those contingent factors are actually concentrated in 'The Strand's 'square black figure', and the ways in which he understood being 'devout'. When John Frederick MacNeice was driven from Omey as a boy (his parents and siblings retreating under a hail of stones) it was for ultimately religious reasons; his own father's work in the (always contentious) Irish Church Missions had rendered him – native to the West as he was – a finally unwelcome visitor on Omey. Interestingly, there were the marks of sectarian conflict on the other side of Louis MacNeice's family, too, for his maternal grandfather, Martin Clesham, had been wounded and incapacitated in violence that also arose from his own Irish Church Missions work. How far this complicated MacNeice's 'nostalgia for a place we had never been' is hard to say; but it is possible to wonder whether the 'flange' and 'belt' his father sees in the Atlantic waves of 'The Strand' are echoing, however remotely, the ready-to-hand fighting tools of a potentially violent reception or send-off. Since the 'mirror of wet sand' reflects both father and son, it is important to ask, more prosaically, how MacNeice saw his father by 1945. Evidence here has to be treated carefully; besides this poem and section VII of 'The Kingdom' in *Springboard* (1944), with its portrait of 'a generous puritan', MacNeice attempted little in the way of an explicit posthumous assessment of the Bishop. There is a certain anti-religious energy in a good deal of his earlier poetry, and there are both sceptical and appreciative remarks from time to time in *The Strings Are False*, the autobiography MacNeice abandoned in 1941, but we should be cautious about taking the son's testimony on historical matters to do with his father entirely at face value.[13] Certainly, the sectarian dimension to this poem's 'square black figure' is an important one; and the poet's catching sight of himself is tinged by this; the Bishop's links with (and indeed origin in) an invasive Protestantism are passed on to his unbelieving son, and the coldness of 'visitors' is one of the truths MacNeice sees in the indifferent 'mirror of wet sand'.

'Time and place,' MacNeice had written (a little stridently) in 'Carrick Revisited', 'our bridgeheads into reality/ But also its concealment!' We do need to remember the time of 'The Strand' as well as its place, for 1945 brought to Achill a MacNeice returned from a War in which the Irish Republic – officially at least – had not been a participant. The tiredness and disillusion of MacNeice's English poems in *Holes in the Sky* are trailing somewhere behind this holidaying visitor in the West; but they are not without their less welcome layers of meaning there, and certainly these are not spoken of, except insofar as 'The Strand' keeps something in itself that is uncompromising – and feels itself to be uncompromised – in the face of a landscape worlds apart from that of post-Blitz London. If we ask ourselves the question of how far MacNeice was his father's son (keeping in mind later poems like 'The Truisms', which set out to engage the father's beliefs with profound respect as well as a sense of mystery), we need to remember that MacNeice himself, as well as his writing, does not provide a clear answer. But in 1945, on Achill, MacNeice was writing work like *The Dark Tower*, the radio play centrally concerned with matters of moral inheritance and public duty, which is in one of its aspects a parable of the trials of the past six years of War, and in which loss is seen in a dual aspect, as sacrifice or waste. This play, which MacNeice conceives during the composition of the poems, insists on the complexity of seeing two things at once; it also, in the end, affirms the necessity of choice and its consequence, action. In 'The Strand', the poet's figure contains something square and black of its own, carrying *The Dark Tower* even while recalling the Bishop carrying his boots.

The Dark Tower is saturated with allusion (to Browning, of course, and to Shakespeare), but one especially strong influence comes from Yeats, and some of his late poetry, notably 'The Black Tower'. 'The Strand', for its part, carries marks of late Yeats in its form – one as unusual for MacNeice in 1945 as it had been for Yeats, when he wrote the *terza rima* lyric, 'Cuchulain Comforted' on his deathbed in 1939. Later on, in the mid-1950s, MacNeice was to engage on the huge *terza rima* enterprise of *Autumn Sequel* – in many ways, though he himself thought otherwise, his least important large-scale work. But 'The Strand' uses *terza rima* not for the purposes of expansion and expansiveness, but – following Yeats's example

---

[13] Ongoing research by the historian David Fitzpatrick, of Trinity College, Dublin, is casting a searching new light on the Bishop's supposed allegiances as a Northern Irish cleric in the early decades of the twentieth century. I am indebted to Professor Fitzpatrick's paper on Bishop MacNeice given at the Louis MacNeice centenary conference, Queen's University Belfast, September 2007.

– for those of concentration and depth. The Yeats poem in the background points up the fact that 'The Strand' is a ghost poem, of sorts, and one about the power (or lack of it) of the dead in their future; in 'Cuchulain Comforted', the hero moves into his posthumous life only to discover that he must become his own opposite. 'The Strand' is not able to cast MacNeice as the opposite of his father – and comes much closer, in fact, to conflating the two mirrored figures – but it is aware of the landscape as something alien or indifferent to both father and son, just as the woods of the world after death demand profound change from Yeats's Cuchulain.

MacNeice's situation in the Achill poems is personal and particular; but it is not only that, if only because of the artistic achievement of a poem like 'The Strand'. The poems are about seeing the self in Ireland, and the complexities and liabilities of this kind of seeing. Another poem, 'Under the Mountain' begins with three short stanzas, each giving a view 'Seen from above', of the sea-foam, a field, and a house. These are then challenged, one by one, in close-up:[14]

> But when you get down
> The breakers are cold scum and the wrack
> Sizzles with stinking life.
>
> When you get down
> The field is a failed or a worth-while crop, the source
> Of back-ache if not heartache.
>
> And when you get down
> The house is a maelstrom of loves and hates where you –
> Having got down – belong.

This is shorthand, perhaps, but still an effective kind of shorthand. MacNeice's own 'belonging', in terms of Ireland or elsewhere, is a question that looks increasingly dated, if only because it presupposes the possibility of a firm and unambiguous answer. But in poetry there are few such things, and it is the subtlety of MacNeice's doubling-up of perspectives which makes the kinds of belonging he imagines so potent and far-reaching. 'Why does your reflection seem/ So lonely?', the question of 'Corner Seat', has different kinds of answer; but the Achill poems are amongst the most interesting and important of these, in their habits of pure (or rather, to use a MacNeice word) impure speculation.

---

[14] Louis MacNeice, *Collected Poems*, p. 268.

Desmond O'Grady

Memories of Louis MacNeice

On a return to Ireland from my studies and teaching years abroad, I decided to spend my summer holidays visiting historical sites in Ireland. When I visited the historically famous harbour town of Kinsale on the southern coast of County Cork – famous for the 1601 Spanish Naval Invasion, with over 3.000 infantry on board, to join the Irish chieftains in their rebellion against the English military occupation of Ireland – I was so delighted with Kinsale town, with its harbour, surroundings and warm climate that I decided to make it my Irish anchorage in Europe.

On this first visit as the guest of a medical doctor, I was introduced to an old pub, The Spaniard, overlooking the harbour and town in an area called Scilly. There, in conversation about my teaching and personal writing life, the doctor asked me if I had read the poems of the outstanding Irish poet Louis MacNeice. I told him I had and that I greatly admired his poems. My host then told me that the poet's widow, Hedli MacNeice, was living on her own in a house slightly down the incline from the pub we were in, and suggested that I, as a poet myself, might visit her in his name as his guest in Kinsale.

The next day I went around to visit her to welcome her to Ireland and to her new home in Kinsale. I presented myself as an admirer of the poems and literary life of her late husband, Louis MacNeice. We chatted about our mutual reasons for being in Kinsale. Then she showed me on her book shelves editions of Louis MacNeice's poems she had brought with her to Kinsale, and she asked me what I had published. In this way we became friends and, because of our mutual interests, we saw each other daily. During these meetings, Hedli showed me the photographs of MacNeice she had hung on the walls of her new home. She also showed me all the manuscripts of the poems, diaries and letters of MacNeice she had brought with her as family treasures. Naturally this discovery in Kinsale was deeply moving to me and it helped me to connect my experiences of those places I had lived in before and was living in now. The development from that was my appreciation of the people of the places, both past and present, and their public. From this epiphany I envisioned a new way to write my poems and began with reading Louis's poems and his personal marginalia.

The following poem was published in 1967 by MacGibbon and Kee Ltd., London, in my collection *The Dark Edge of Europe*. Since then it has been re-published in my collected poems: *The Road Taken 1956-1996* (University of Salzburg Press, Austria 1996).

Reading the Unpublished Manuscripts of Louis MacNeice at Kinsale Harbour

One surely tires eventually of the frequent references – the gossip,
praise, the blame, the intimate anecdote – to those
who, for one unpredictable reason or other (living

abroad, difference of age, chance, the friends one chose,
being detained too long at the most opportune moment) one
never, face to tactile face, has met; but who
had the way things fall fallen favourably, once met, for some
right physic force, would have been polar, kindred you –
though time, space, human nature, sometimes contract
to force the action done that makes abstraction fact.

Here in this mock of a room which might have been yours, might have been
the place of our eventual meeting, I find a berth temporarily
(so long too late) among your possessions.

                                        Alone, except for your face
in the framed photos, I sit, with your manuscripts spread over my knees,
reliving the unpublished truths of your autobiography.
On the shelves and table, desk, floor, your books
and papers, your bundles of letters – as if you were just moving in
or out, or had been already for years –
like a poem in the making you'll never now finish.
Through the window I see down to the hook of Old Kinsale Harbour.
Mid-summer. Under the sun the sea as smooth as a dish.
Below on the quays the fishermen wind up the morning's business:
stacking the fishboxes, scraping the scales from their tackle and hands.
Behind this house the hills shovel down on the town's slate roofs
the mysterious green mounds of their history.
Flaming fir, clouted holly.
Not an Irish harbour at all, but some other –
the kind you might find along the Iberian coast, only greener.

Down to here, down to this clay of contact between us, Hugh O'Neill
                                        once marched
from way up your part of the country, the North, the winter of sixteen
hundred and one, to connect with the long needed Spaniards three months
under siege in the Harbour. Having played the English at their own game
                                        and watched
all his life for his moment, he lost our right lot in one bungled night
and with it the thousands of years of our past and our future. He began
what divides the North they brought your ash back to, from the South I
                                        have left
for Rome – where O'Neill's buried exiled. And here, then, this moment, late
as the day is (what matter your physical absence) I grow towards your
                                        knowing,
towards the reassurance of life in mortality, the importance, the value
                                        of dying.

Dennis O'Driscoll

Michael Hamburger
1924 – 2007

If I knew the world would end tomorrow,
I would plant an apple tree today.
> Martin Luther

Time and again, you believed the world –
unmade by man – was doomed to end soon.
Yet you went on tending apple trees,
tempted always by the endangered varieties.

You, who grew up in a world ending at the infernal
platform where all railroads led, all cattle
trucks converged, had been transplanted
to where apple blossoms promised a fresh start.

And whenever our planet was on the brink,
ready to break up in disarray, you saved its skin
by planting further apple saplings, digging in
with Devonshire Quarrenden grown from pips,

adding Norfolk Royal Russet, Coe's Golden Drop –
tilted with moss and mistletoe – to the balance,
preserving fruit spurned on grounds of taste,
non-standard shapes, unapproved core values.

Your trees, surviving you, arrive on time –
as ever – this year, freighted with rare species.
And each windfall is a pebble planted on
the gravestone of the man who, sparing

even one life from extinction, saved the world.

Will Stone

Unpicked Apples: Memories of Michael Hamburger

i

It is distressing enough enduring a sudden bereavement when announced through relatives or friends, but when one is requested by a national newspaper to provide an obituary for a cherished friend whom you were under the impression was still alive, it elevates the grievous situation to an almost insupportable level of pathos. But this is indeed how I learned a few days later, of the death of my near neighbour and friend the poet Michael Hamburger, who died during the morning of 7th June 2007. Needless to say I was unable to respond in the affirmative to the functional request and fortunately the task was passed to somebody else, who in any case was far better equipped than I to carry out such a labour. What made matters worse was that I was at that moment miles away from East Suffolk in the south of France at the centre for literary translators in Arles. There I sat at my computer in the college library stunned by this brief sterile email that carried such a weight of implication. Before long a number of fellow translators of all nationalities parked nearby realised something was wrong and made tentative enquiries. When I explained in a rather decrepit monologue, my voice shaky with shock, they became respectfully silent. What could they say anyway; they had not encountered Michael Hamburger, largely because they were Finnish and Czech, Lebanese or Russian and most were working on novels or crime fiction. They did not know that the most prolific translator of German poetry into English of the modern age had suddenly died without warning, a man whose titanic oeuvre had, one could argue, some bearing on virtually all translated European literature of the last sixty years. Nor were they aware he was a unique poet of the natural world, a genuine poet, not an academic or critic merely calling himself one, a poet who had imbued his translations with the full measure of his voluminous reading, his own poetic impulse and sensitive linguistic judgements. Like one of the post war giants he brought to the UK, Paul Celan, he moved with natural grace between the art of translation and the creation of his own poems. Nor did they know he was an exile who had never had the acclaim he deserved in his adopted country England, whose island bound literary culture he had, like a doctor hoping in vain for vital signs, given shot after shot of both the principal and lesser known German language poets of the twentieth century, but was by contrast something of a revered master in his native Germany from which his family, being Jewish, had fled in the years of Nazi persecution. No, they knew none of this, but they understood in the most basic humane way that I was catastrophically felled. Presently, a cup of tea was gently placed at my side without a word. In recognition that existent language was merely an unwelcome gawper at such an event, this simple gesture, which of course has its very English overtones, seemed peculiarly sufficient and touching.

Soon I had booked my flights back to the UK for the funeral which took place a week later at Middleton church. Like many others painfully awakened by this sudden loss, I wrote to his wife, the poet Anne Beresford, a letter which despite the powerful emotions and feeling decanted into it seemed to become more and more uncomfortable and restless as it lengthened, as if the language were looking back with some embarrassment, as if in the enormity of what had happened it had lost confidence in itself and were only making a pretence of what it had been charged with delivering.

In these early days of bereavement I could not help but recall another sudden death five years earlier and the way the news of that grim event was relayed to me by Michael himself. In mid December 2001, I arrived home to find a message on my answer phone. 'Will, I'm afraid I have some very bad news. Max has been killed in a car accident outside Norwich.' Michael gave no sweetener, no lead-in or solemn epilogue, merely the information required with its message as sudden and as sharp as a fall through ice into frozen water, made all the more harrowing for its clinical and inescapable truth. This brief statement announced a deep despair felt keenly by all who had come into the writer, WG Sebald's orbit. This perverse event deleted not only an extraordinary reader and unclassifiable writer of rare faculty, but a man who had for many become a symbol of something even more precious, though more obscure, which stemmed from that gift, the essence of which descended like a shroud over friends, colleagues and pupils during that now blighted Christmas period. This younger German exile almost inevitably became a close friend of Michael's. They chose the same region in which to reside, were naturally high yielding farmers of a European literary heritage, notably of course in the German/Austrian area, whose stock held an abundance of existential enquiry that remained and still remains to a large extent utterly alien to the Anglophone reader. As writer exiles they recognised and respected each other with that coercive intuitive instinct which fashions life-long friendships between certain individuals, in their case a friendship consolidated by Michael's last great translation work, his exemplary translations of Max's now celebrated long poem 'After Nature'. Max's inclusion of Michael in his book *The Rings of Saturn* has led to a growing interest in his life, culminating in a procession of film-makers and Sebald inspired pilgrims from across Europe arriving at Marsh Acres. Max's account of a visit there in which he relates a sense of blurring between Michael's existence and his own, was illustrated by two photographs, one of which showed a tapering pile of used envelopes and jiffy bags in limbo, destined for re-use or possible destruction. This haphazard structure basking in its organic authenticity, yet somehow concealing an as yet undefined purpose, clearly drew Max's eye both visually and symbolically. The other photo shows the chair and desk at which Michael used to work in the library. This long deserted desk was for as long as I can remember covered in one corner by an irresistibly photogenic mound of abandoned spectacle cases, a sight thankfully now captured for posterity by one of the stills from Tacita Deane's short film about Michael which appeared in the Norwich-based *Waterlogged* exhibition earlier this year.

I also remember an exchange following his attendance at Max's funeral in Norfolk in which Michael sought to express the severity of the sudden loss of Max, to articulate the onerous sense of vacancy left by his passing, which was that much more than the premature loss of a well-loved creative man in late middle age. I always had the feeling from his often guarded reverence for Max that Michael realised astutely the true reach and sacrifice of Sebald's vision, not only the writings that had made him an icon in the Anglophone world, but the the painstaking assemblage of an entire work through long gestation, the vital consequence of his uncompromising labour of literary absorption, the true value such invisible heroism had in today's lavishly self-referencing media-saturated climate. With a restrained emotion which made the appropriate dignified backdrop to his words, he said how a light really had been extinguished with Max's passing and it seemed, as he put it, as if the world had 'visibly darkened'. This was no rhetoric about the dying of the light or a candle snuffed, but Michael sought to express how in some way the light really had dimmed, that some unique flowering could never be replaced, that communal extinction flexed with anticipation at the moment Max left the road. Michael said little but felt more, that was always my feeling. I imagine he distrusted resorting to words of lofty emotion, which, in their race to lower the wreaths before a catastrophic event, can irreparably damage that incubus of ingenious silence in which the truth is shyly forming.

Michael's funeral at Middleton parish church was, as one would expect, well attended. I arrived early for fear of not securing a seat, but found only the Middleton sheep in numbers contentedly cropping the churchyard grass behind their little electric fence. But, before long, mourners from near and far had respectfully shoe-horned themselves into the tiny pews of the church to hear a simple and poignant service backed by an accomplished choral ensemble, which gradually unfurled the sensitivity and forethought of those who had designed it. Fellow poet and translator, Oliver Bernard, read with a keen sense of conviction a most relevant quote by E.M. Forster. Here it is in full:

I believe in an aristocracy of the sensitive,
the considerate and the plucky.
Its members are to be found in all nations
and classes, and all through the ages,
and there is a secret understanding when they meet.
They represent the true human tradition,
the one permanent victory over cruelty and chaos.

The dignified murmur of approval which followed this address served to illustrate the esteem in which Michael was held as one who had 'laboured' (a term he often used himself, especially concerning the garden and which like other endearing archaisms, revealed his German language roots) against those materialist eruptions of the modern world which threatened to annihilate the spirit. On his dyke-enclosed island of Marsh Acres, Michael had retreated, the vicar explained, to observe more attentively the natural world, which for him held both promise of transcendence from human folly, Mammon's most noxious vapours and the ever more vulgar comportment of fellow beings increasingly severed from their natural surroundings by the manic sprouting of technology. More was said on such a theme and fortunately the man of God managed to restrain from any of the ecclesiastical rhetoric which, like a vigorous ivy, habitually overwhelms the pulpit on such occasions. At the closing of the ceremony, Anthony Rudolf stepped forward tentatively from the choir. Gifted essayist and publisher, Rudolf was, along with Peter Jay, Michael's own publisher, one of that modest but vital band who set up their poetry presses in the late sixties and garnered the support, respect and friendship of their literary elder. Having donned his skull cap, Rudolf announced that he would now read the Kaddish, the Jewish prayer for the dead. Although the Hebrew was unintelligible to most people present, the smoke of music that drifted off the language began to tell. I looked at the pall bearers and their impassive faces, their well-groomed silver hair, men of late middle age waiting for the signal to depart under the light rain of that lilting Kaddish. Even they seemed moved. That the service ended with a language we did not know but somehow comprehended communally in that moment, somehow seemed to me a most appropriate and fateful nod to the ever mysterious art of translation and its legacy of minor miracles.

ii

Mid October 2007. Yesterday afternoon on one of those all too rare mild days of autumnal sun, I once more visited Marsh Acres, the Suffolk home of Michael Hamburger for three decades. The wild garden he had created and which had sustained Michael in the end threatened to overwhelm him physically. Today, however, it seemed to be aware of an opportunity to perform a slow procession of its maturing achievements. The sensory spectacle delivered by the decay of fruit and leaves tenderly governed by the late sun was irresistible. One could not help thinking of Hölderlin's memorable image of 'yellow pears hanging in the lake' from the poem 'The Half of Life', as the sun warmed the skin of the fallen blemished fruits held with such devotion and acceptance of impermanence in that charitable vestibule to extinction formed by the rugged tussocks of grass. Nearby the massed pots of geraniums still roared on, their ancient pots gradually losing their outline to the meadow grass licking their flanks, and vast beds dominated by shrub roses seemed to be pushing out ever further into the lawn as if taking advantage before the winter thinned them out and sank its portcullis on further growth. Unseen from here yet not far distant lay the orchard, protected by a massive beech hedge barrier with a single mouse hole opening, where, on passing through, one experienced a vague seasoning of romantic anticipation. On the other side, an area largely left to its own devices, an enclosure concerned with its own slow maturation, furnishing its fruits as if a by-product, off-cuts of some greater obscure labour which one may gather in baskets and store in lines if one chooses, as Michael did, forming pleasurable mosaics of yellow gold and green gold, red flushes, rough skin and smooth with brown pitting and the odd wormhole. Or leave them there a little longer in their unbearably tight bunches, turning them gently next time to see if they release. One or two do, they are ready to depart. These trees are so heavily laden now with apples which will mostly now remain un-picked. Our modest basket is soon filled with many different and rare varieties whose exotic names we do not know, but can only wildly guess, *Orleans Renette*? I enquire, knocking the wall of the highly taut slightly tacky skin of the fruit with my knuckle for the pleasure of the woody sound. But we have no real idea, we are trespassers here. Every time I enter this area I feel I should exhibit some sign of reverence, for there is a holiness here, but not a religious one, the holiness of the wheel that has completed its turn and in the right direction, the simple path of labour and reward, a chance to recline in the loop of reclusive non-interference. Still more trees where great clusters hang defiantly on their rope branches like sailors in a storm, waiting for our outstretched hands to test their readiness, to relieve them, old players they seem already though merely a season old, their hoary skins and idle rotundity, wholly rustic apples innocently redolent with authenticity, like those Cézanne made famous and which an intoxicated Rilke likened to 'those found in the pocket of an old countryman's jacket'. It was Michael who wore that jacket for three decades and whose rough soil-loving hands reached up for those apples and carried them into the house to ripen, to breathe, in the parlour like room between the library and lounge, where they formed their cheerful rows and ranks, their random spirals and pirouettes of colour, their dumpy majesty. Depicted in one of the photographs in Sebald's *The Rings of Saturn*, they finally achieved fame.

I had the privilege of knowing Michael and his wife Anne for a third of the period in which they resided in Suffolk. In those early days I was invited to Sunday lunch at the long table in the kitchen. Many of the good folk who shared that table are now sadly gone, namely Jane and Elizabeth, Anne's two sisters. But then my 'slot' became tea-time and most weeks I would spend an hour or two in the company of the Hamburgers. Michael would always have green tea with a dash of milk. He made this himself in his own pot and usually gathered his tea-making paraphernalia on an old wooden tray which went to and from his living room to the kitchen, making the daily journey in the same way each day no matter the season. This was one element in the microcosm of Michael's working life which followed a set pattern, enabling him to work uninterrupted at the same hours each day. The morning was work from an early hour, letter-writing always and other pressing literary matters. The afternoon was brief rest, reading or rather re-reading, listening to music, pottering in the garden and receiving visitors such as myself. When I arrived Anne was usually first to greet me and then would have to inform Michael of my arrival. If he was watching a sporting event of some importance, his arrival might be slower than usual, but he would then come through the door briskly in that slightly forward-leaning but robust manner. Often when I arrived I would hear the delicate sound of the piano drifting out from the lounge and I would come upon Anne absorbed in playing. Quiet as possible, I would settle myself down to wait until she finished the piece or noticed my presence. Gradually these visits at the fag end of the afternoon found their own rhythm and served as an opportunity to gripe communally at catastrophic events, exchange literary news and so on. But they were also a chance to air stories from the past, memories of long-waned or rekindled literary associations, trips past and present to Austria and Germany for readings, amusing anecdotes about writers they had known in the Hampstead years, gifted poets who had died young and now are utterly forgotten, tales of those eccentrics who pester authors with letters and reams of their own unhinged work. But also at these tea ceremonies, I was presented with books from Michael's library, something he thought would interest me particularly, or something he had recently acquired from Germany. Suddenly he would be gone and then return with some beautifully-bound collection or rare art book, sometimes his father's finely bound books of German poets and writers and once, when I was most fortunate, the letters of Paul Celan. Sitting one afternoon in Michael's house, I handled those tiny yellowing envelopes containing Celan's correspondence to his English translator despatched from Paris in the 1960s. Staring at the faded purplish typewriter ink, I felt peculiarly privileged to know this extraordinary 'importer of overlooked genius' who was standing beside me monitoring my reaction.

For those ten years of visiting Marsh Acres, the approach and entrance options to the house remained unchanged. A choice of two parking places, one next to the wooden gate swung back between the now burgeoning fig tree and the old Nissan hut which billeted soldiers in the war, or on the shorter steep drive where one can either approach the house at the side as would a tradesmen of yester year, or if fine from the garden at the rear, passing the long narrow glass house, rebuilt a few years before and never in Michael's eyes able to equal the noble wreck it replaced. This was my preferred route to the house, especially in the summer months as one would more often than not be ushered through by the easeful scent of the meandering box hedges and happen upon the 'Hölderlin pump', so named because the date of 1770 embossed in its metal housing was the year of the poet's birth. In the little pond beneath it, dark frogs rested their jerking chins mournfully against the weed-fringed stone. Three, four, now five months on from his death, there is a little initially at least to show Michael has departed. Some of the bushes which clustered around the great bay window behind which he worked have been cut back to allow in more light and at the front of the house, and more of the unrelieved vegetation has gone to let walls pestered by damp Suffolk winters breathe again. A small apple tree I had never noticed now stands rather surprised with a yew's dark canopy shading it from the road. The house seems more vast than ever in its new-found nakedness, but somehow relieved also to feel its foundations again. Michael never wanted to cut anything down unless absolutely necessary. He did not care for peripheral 'functional' activity around him, change that would disturb him, interruptions of a purely domestic character and preferred to let things grow and decay as they would if man was not continually hounding them and trying to contain them. But inadvertently over the years, for the beautiful bay window, this was to prove a near death sentence. Now, thankfully, it is to be fully restored at the eleventh hour, reprieved from a slow extinction solemnly endured behind the myriad fans of jiffy bags and envelopes, the letters and general literary detritus that accumulates so naturally on the shore of a writer's desk. Michael liked the idea, I think, that nature was closing in and could not be dissuaded from its path. Often he would remark on this inevitability and does so in the opening frames of the film by Frank Wierke, *Michael Hamburger – An English Poet from Germany*, as he fights his way though the 'insanely sprouting' creepers of the marsh garden, realising that he too must accept that he can no longer prevent the swallowing up of the area he has tended by the more forceful plants, who have their own mysterious agenda. There was a comfort perhaps and a necessary romantic reclusive indulgence in letting the overhung or hidden path not be cleared and made navigable by continual human straining against fate.

As usual when someone dies we conduct a stream of images of them, images that return again and again, bringing still others with them. Many of those regarding Michael are so routine yet somehow poignant, such as the way he used to prepare the fire in his living room and study early on in the day, so that when I visited around mid afternoon, a nest of mossy twigs collected from the lawn stood high over the grate, ready to see off the evening chill. I will always remember entering that room and seeing Michael in his reading chair bent over a book on which his hand rested, keeping the page from turning, or watching some sporting contest on the television with the sound down, because he could no longer bear the inane commentary. Sadly Michael's generation is now all but gone. He was one of the last and he spoke often in the later years about friends falling away one by one. But I felt Michael would somehow outlive us all, despite the irrationality of such a statement. Though of modest build, he always seemed so tough and wiry, on his hands and knees again in the garden pulling out vagrant grass stems from beds or puffing through the undergrowth with his bundle of sticks, his old blue corduroy jacket decked with seeds and the stains of moss. But his departure came suddenly and surprised us all.

Without meaning to sound trite or sentimental, the loss of Michael represents for me the final separation of the soulless media-fostered industrial combine of today's literary activity from that distinguished and, somehow more outwardly at least, 'civilised' generation of, for want of a better expression, we might call 'men of letters', the last survivors of a time when replying to letters and behaving in a sympathetic and reasonable manner were still deemed preferable to the prancing ego-mania and barbarous self-interest flaunted today. Michael was an exception, however, in this regard, replying to his correspondents immediately and often at length, showing concern and sensitivity. He also felt a responsibility to younger poets and budding translators who wrote to him and he replied to them with encouragement and affection. Across the decades he grafted at these replies and all manner of other literary work on a bewildering variety of manual typewriters. Olivetti, Adler, Corona…they all graced his desk at some time or another and then were replaced due to a broken key, an obsolete ribbon or a failure to supply certain German characters. After Michael's death these typewriters ended up neatly stacked under the main staircase at Marsh Acres. I was honoured to be allowed to keep one in Michael's memory. As I opened each box, revealing the antiquated machines, these heavily armoured workhorses of all different makes and periods, the sheer historic weight of Michael's long career sunk in. A writer's life, there, under the stairs, waiting to be distributed, remnants seeking new homes, finding new tributaries. These tired machines propping each other up, totally obsolete, more so than quill and pen, I observed for some time with a mixture of sorrow and admiration. As for technological 'upgrading', Michael never touched a computer, nor for that matter did Max Sebald, who I recall dryly indicating to me the plastic wrapping still around the plug of the one delivered to his office in late 2001. I admired the refusal by these white-haired elders to be prised from their tradition and an acknowledgement that the manner of writing and the tools which imbue it with a certain flavouring or feeling (if only for the writer) are sacrosanct. There is something more pure and self-contained about writing without electricity, without artificial aids, without word processing, the duplicitous interference of technology, though naturally sheer practicality for most writers has overtaken any other considerations. We all succumb in the end, but I am glad Michael never did. The only concession he made was to install a modest and somewhat archaic photocopier in the store room next to his apples.

iii

November, 2007. The poet Paul Stubbs has come to stay and we are on our way back from the Aldeburgh Poetry Festival. My companion asks to visit Michael's grave and we arrive at Middleton church as the light is beginning to fade. A short walk through the churchyard brings us to the tree-lined avenue off which Michael was laid to rest. Last here on a mild June day in a throng of mourners, I could not be quite sure of the grave's location in the gathering gloom, but a fresher mound with a tunic of grassy tussocks and a single geranium at its head seemed the likely spot. However, there appeared to be no cross in evidence to confirm this and out loud I said how strange this was, bending down to look for the remains of a temporary one. As we stood either side of the grave, I sensed a movement and heard the murmur of voices approaching from beneath the low hanging trees. A man and woman appeared and greeted us with 'Are you looking for Mr Hamburger?' 'Yes, he is here I think,' I replied, or words to that effect. The man who spoke in a broad Suffolk accent stated that they too were here for Mr Hamburger and at the same time raised from beside him a modest wooden cross with a sharpened point.

Squatting down, he rammed it into the ground at the head of the grave. 'There we go, then,' he said. 'Now people will be able to find him.' He then bade us farewell and the local couple retreated as suddenly as they had arrived. It seemed rather odd that we had picked the exact moment to come to the grave and that I had spoken about the absence of a cross. Then, literally as I spoke, one arrived. I felt this was a good omen and as darkness descended we departed, our feet making little sound as we sank into a range of fresh molehills before finding the firmer sheep-cropped turf of the path. I reflected as we walked back to the car how Michael would have savoured to the full this country churchyard in November with its tenant crew of crows and damp aromatic leaf fall, a churchyard he knew so well. Like Robert Walser, he understood that there was no need to travel huge distances to trigger a writer's inspiration, but with the right kind of eye, one could merely take a fifteen minute walk down the lane from one's house and be exposed to natural wonders that could glut the mind for a lifetime. When I got home, I encountered the poem 'Echoes', from his last book of poems entitled *Circling the Square*, a collection which in the melée of new titles has been largely ignored, despite the fact that it harbours some very fine work. The third section of the poem seems particularly apposite and I quote it here. This poem like many others of its kind returns again and again with migrant intuition to that same undying source, funnelled through the Marsh garden, ensuring Michael's distinctive voice will continue to resonate despite the dominance of those vaguely coalescing cliques which hierarchically groom each other in the increasingly squalid arena of today's poetry 'business'.

Echoes III

November now, half moon
Clear in cleansed air, colder,
So desultory then the sunshine
That even by noon to us
It seemed as unemployed
As the showers in between
On to leaves falling fast
From boughs not yet bare.

If an order ruled it was
The wind's, only the wind's
That rips a green leaf free,
Shivers a slanted beam
Through the leaved boughs bending,
Shakes raindrops down from these
To make food of the fallen,
Feed the still standing tree.

Wolfgang Görtschacher

Against Prejudice and Ignorance:
Michael Hamburger's Celebration of
German Literature in the United States

'Whatever the advantages of free imitation for other kinds of verse, poetry as austere as most of this translated here quite naturally calls for a corresponding austerity on the translator's part [...]. Where the original text is less austere and more playful [...] faithfulness not only permits but demands a greater measure of independence. [...] Adaptation, transposition, invention, then, are simply part of faithfulness in the rendering of poems, though it is the character of any one poem that suggests how much of these is required. [...] to use the originals as pretexts for original composition would have offended against the integrity of the poets.'[1]

Preliminaries

I have neither been able to consult the Michael Hamburger Archive at the Harry Ransom Humanities Research Centre situated at the Department of Germanic Languages at the University of Texas, Austin, nor have I had time to work in Hamburger's own study in his Suffolk house. The former contains Hamburger's studies and translations of Hugo von Hofmannsthal, proofs of translations of Georg Büchner, Paul Celan, Johann Wolfgang von Goethe, Günter Grass, Hofmannsthal, Hölderlin, and Nelly Sachs, and some correspondence. The latter is the only other substantial collection of Hamburger material to speak of. A further archive of potential interest, the Carcanet and *PN Review* archive in Manchester, is no longer available. All the relevant records at the former headquarters of his – until the early 1990s – main publisher, such as correspondence, sales figures, contracts with Hamburger's American publishers, etc. were destroyed in the IRA bombing of Manchester in 1996.

However, I corresponded with Hamburger for some time from 1997-1998. I also met him in Austria at the Rauris Literature Festival on 21 March 1998 – one day ahead of his 74th birthday – when I conducted a 120-minute interview with the poet-translator. In the 1960s and 1970s in particular, when Hamburger held posts as lecturer and visiting professor at a great number of US universities, he published regularly, both his own poetry as well as translations, in a great variety of literary magazines, such as *Partisan Review, Hudson Review, The Boston University Journal,* and *Poetry Chicago.*

---

[1] Michael Hamburger, ed., 'Introduction', *East German Poetry: An Anthology* (Oxford: Carcanet, 1972) xxi.

70

Hamburger's Various Artistic Masks – the Translator-Editor

Where does one start when analysing the influence one individual person has exercised on the reception of German Literature in America? Every critic must be conscious of the fact that in most cases he has only access to insignificant external characteristics, such as reviews in specialised magazines which, more often than not, have nothing to do with the actual reception of a book among the reading public, and letters to the editors of such magazines. Remarks in autobiographies or books of criticism may give some impression of the particular influence a writer or a book of translation has had on the career of an individual colleague. If fortunate, one may even persuade publishers to look up their statistics, if available, and provide hard facts such as print-runs and sales figures. Nonetheless, these superficialities do not throw light on the reception process that takes place between a book and its (wider) readership. A writer's reputation in a country other than his own depends almost entirely on the ability and taste of his translators, provided that this particular author's work is selected for translation in the first place. A translator-editor not only influences the reception process by the way in which he translates a text, but also what he considers worth translating. The smaller the market – the number of translators and translations – is, the greater the extent the influence of particular translator-editors can be felt, which may result in false heroes and strange gods, i.e., an over representation of particular authors in foreign countries which does not correspond with the real stature of their work. On the other hand, translator-editors may even resurrect authors from oblivion, as is the case with Hamburger and Franz Baermann Steiner, never recognized in the German-speaking countries.[2] The authors selected by Hamburger have been fortunate in their translator.

Hamburger seems to have influenced the American reception of German Literature on various levels: as translator, as editor of anthologies, as critic, and as poet. His first major book to appear in the States was *Beethoven: Letters, Journals, and Conversations*, which was published by Pantheon Books (New York) together with the London press Thames & Hudson in 1951. The former was directed by Kurt Wolff, an eminent German emigré publisher, who in 1961 founded his Helen & Kurt Wolff Books imprint, which he edited as a specialist list within the big Harcourt Brace Jovanovich publishing conglomerate. In 1953, Wolff published Hamburger's first Hölderlin collection to appear in the States entitled *Hölderlin: His Poems*, whose British edition had been issued by Harvill Press one year earlier. It is a revised and enlarged edition of *Poems* published in 1943, of which Hamburger says that it

---

[2] Franz Baermann Steiner, 'Six Poems,' trans. Michael Hamburger, *PN Review* 87 (Sept.-Oct. 1992) 38-39; *Modern Poetry in Translation* 2 (New Series, Autumn 1992, special bilingual Franz Baermann Steiner issue).

came out far too early, when I was too young. All I had was enthusiasm, but no knowledge. I did not even understand the metres of Hölderlin's poems and so I translated them into free verse. When I was in the army from 1943 to 1947 I reworked these translations and added new ones as well. First I found the Harvill Press, who published it in England. As I was already in touch with Wolff I must have mentioned it to him that this book was coming out and he took it over.[3]

Hölderlin: His Poems, with prose translations below the original, was reviewed by Lisel Mueller, a poet and translator of Brecht, in the January 1963 issue of *Poetry* (Chicago). In this very favourable review the critic stresses that Hamburger 'presents us with a fair and generous selection of Hölderlin's poems [...] includ[ing] all the famous expansive poems from the middle period [...]. It is in these poems that the diction [...] becomes extremely difficult with its inverted syntax, incremental appended clauses, and ambiguous usage of single words.'[4] Fourteen years later University of Michigan Press at Ann Arbor printed Hamburger's – once again – revised edition entitled *Poems and Fragments*. This happened through the mediation of the poet Donald Hall, who had, together with his co-editors Robert Pack and Louis Simpson, included some of Hamburger's own poems in the anthology *New Poets of England and America* (Cleveland: Meridian, 1957). Many of the revisions included in the Michigan Press edition had already been incorporated by Hamburger into Penguin's *Selected Poems* published in 1961.

The same year Bollingen Foundation published Hugo von Hofmannsthal's *Poems and Verse Plays*, edited by Hamburger, in their Bollingen Series. In *A Mug's Game: Intermittent Memoirs 1924-1954*, Hamburger reports the following about the difficulties involved in the publication of this volume:

Early in the new year [1951] I got down to work on the Beethoven book. At the same time Stephen Spender telephoned, suggesting that he and I collaborate over the Hofmannsthal translations he was doing for the Bollingen Foundation. A line-by-line collaboration proved impossible. Each of us translated different works. After complications of various kinds, and the lapse of nearly a decade, the editorship was offered to me. Since that was a way of breaking the deadlock, I accepted, with Stephen's generous consent.[5]

---

[3] Michael Hamburger, personal interview, 21 March 1998.
[4] Lisel Mueller, 'Four German Poets,' rev. of *Goethe's Faust*, Part I and sections from Part II, trans. and ed. Walter Kaufmann; *Hölderlin*, trans. and ed. Michael Hamburger; *Selected Letters of Rainer Maria Rilke*, ed. Harry T. Moore, *Poetry* (Chicago) 101.4 (January 1963): 289. [287-92]
[5] Michael Hamburger, *A Mug's Game: Intermittent Memoirs 1924-1954* (Cheadle: Carcanet, 1973) 251.

Spender contributed translations to the present volume, as did Hamburger, which finally included 23 lyrics and six verse plays, mostly written during Hofmannsthal's early youth, in the 1890s, with complete German texts facing the English, and a preface by T. S. Eliot. Lisel Mueller, in her review printed in *Poetry* (Chicago), obviously pays attention to the American readers' ignorance of Hofmannsthal and provides useful background information to the period covered by the present volume. But she also refers to particular difficulties the Hofmannsthal translators had to face up to:

> The various translators do an able job with the unrhymed material, but often run afoul of rhyme and metre, when they try to reproduce it in English. Hofmannsthal frequently uses rhyming verbs, and since the verb, in German, normally occurs at the end of a clause or sentence, this works out well, but carried over into English, it produces an effect of awkward inversion and 'poetic' rhetoric. Then, too, in a perfectly scanning translation, there is always the need to add words to fill out the line – German words generally requiring more syllables than the corresponding English ones – and these extra words, usually adjectives, are superfluous and sometimes confusing.[6]

In 1963 Bollingen Foundation published another Hofmannsthal volume edited by Hamburger entitled *Selected Plays and Libretti*, which contains three plays and three libretti: *Electra* (trans. Alfred Schwarz), *The Salzburg Great Theatre of the World* (trans. Vernon Watkins), *The Cavalier of the Rose* (trans. Christopher Holme), *Arabella* (trans. Nora Wydenbruck and Christopher Middleton), *The Difficult Man*, which Edwin Muir 'had wanted to translate before he became ill'[7] and was finally translated by Willa Muir, and Hamburger himself contributed his rendering of the sombre tragedy *The Tower*. Both volumes were distributed by Pantheon Books, who – as was already mentioned – published Hamburger's first book of translation in the States. In 1970 Princeton University Press published the editor's introductions to the two volumes of Hofmannsthal's Selected Works separately as a critical book entitled *Hofmannsthal: Three Essays*, which, Hamburger stresses, was taken quite seriously by Hofmannsthal scholars.

Günter Grass the novelist had been introduced to an American audience with Ralph Manheim's rendering of *The Tin Drum*, published by Pantheon in 1963. While John Simon, in his review for *Partisan Review*, considers Grass's novel a German approximation of *Ulysses*, he slaughters Manheim's translation:

> It is to be deplored that *The Tin Drum* comes to English readers diminished by Ralph Manheim's translation: in length, by well over a hundred pages;

---

[6] Lisel Mueller, 'Four German Poets' 289-90.
[7] Hamburger, *The Mug's Game* 252.

in quality, inestimably. Much that was either too difficult, or seemed too elaborate or obscene, has been flattened out, abridged, or omitted. On almost every page constructions, jokes, meanings are weakened, disregarded, or missed. None of which, however, has kept the translation from being extolled by literary and academic reviewers alike.[8]

His American reputation as a poet, however, Grass almost exclusively owes to Hamburger and Middleton. At a time when Grass had only published two collections of poetry, *Die Vorzüge der Windhühner* (1956) and *Glasdreieck* (1960), Hamburger and Middleton collected their translations of Grass's poems to be published as *Selected Poems* by Helen & Kurt Wolff Books (New York) in 1966. Four of Hamburger's translations had been included in *Modern German Poetry 1910-1960: An Anthology with Verse Translations*, issued by New York's Grove Press in 1962. Hamburger did not approach Grass when arranging the latter's bi-lingual *Selected Poems*: 'It would not have been any good sending him the early translations, because I do not think he knew any English to speak of at the time. Now he knows a bit of English, but even so I do not think he would want to be bothered with checking the translations.'[9] Anthony Hecht, who reviewed it for *The Hudson Review*, welcomes its publication, describing Grass as 'an excellent poet', who

deals with fantasy, irony, humor, and of his predecessors seems most to resemble Erich Kästner and Bertolt Brecht, though his irony is less savage and crude than Brecht's. The translations [...] should not have been remarkably difficult to do, for Grass writes in a rather free form, and none of the poems included here employ rhyme; and on the whole the translators seem pretty well to have succeeded, though there are moments of odd awkwardness. [...] Even so, Grass is a pleasure to read, even in translation.[10]

Lisel Mueller, in her review for *Poetry* (Chicago), states that Grass 'falls into the category of poets who "work" in English, and Michael Hamburger and Christopher Middleton prove so in their translation.'[11] She characterises Grass's poems as 'structures of specific, concrete, everyday speech imposed on bizarre backgrounds'.

---

[8] John Simon, 'The Drummer of Danzig', rev. of *The Tin Drum*, by Günter Grass, trans. Ralph Manheim, *Partisan Review* 30.3 (Fall 1963): 452. [446-53]

[9] Hamburger, personal interview.

[10] Anthony Hecht, 'Poetry Chronicle', rev. of *Poets on Poetry*, by Howard Nemerov; *Nights and Day*, by James Merrill; *A Joyful Noise*, by Donald Finkel; *Winter News*, by John Haines; *Poems*, by Jon Silkin; *Wildtrack*, by John Wain; *Selected Poems*, by Günter Grass, *The Hudson Review* 19.2 (Summer 1966): 338. [330-38]

[11] Lisel Mueller, 'German Chronicle', rev. of *Contemporary German Poetry, An Anthology*, trans. and ed. Gertrude Clorius Schwebell; *Selected Poems*, by Günter Grass, trans. Michael Hamburger and Christopher Middleton; *Manual of Piety (Die Hauspostille)*, by Bertold Brecht, trans. Eric Bentley, *Poetry* (Chicago) 111.5 (February 1968): 338. [336-40]

Mueller goes beyond Hecht's categorizing by calling him 'witty, brilliant, angry'. To the American readership she introduces Grass as

> the moralist exposing our cupidity and stupidity, but he does it playfully, by showing us grotesqueries, odd juxtapositions. Folding chairs embody homelessness and dislocation; spoons are the curved shape of experience; situations that have been surrounded by sentiment are suddenly, and shockingly, seen in a vacuum. His surrealism can be obscure, but more often it comes frighteningly close. And he is capable also of the bitterly plain and brief statement [...].[12]

At the time Middleton had, more or less, dropped out as Grass's translator, and this is why later collections, with one exception, have been translated by Hamburger exclusively. In 1969 it was again Helen & Kurt Wolff Books who published the bilingual collection *New Poems*, Hamburger's translation of Grass's third collection *Ausgefragt (Questioned)*. R.H.W. Dillard, in his review for *The Kenyon Review*, found the collection 'as interesting and admirable as the earlier *Selected Poems*'. In the reviewer's opinion, 'the book does achieve a dawn, a March in its own way, but its journey is bleak and surprising, as blunt as the fist Grass drew to burst from the dust jacket. Its poetry is as vital as Eberhart's, as honest as McAfee's.'[13] In April 1977 the same press published *In the Egg and Other Poems*, which included on its 143 pages most of the older and some new translations by Hamburger and the handful of Middleton's translations from Grass's first American volume. Since then they have issued *Drawings & Words 1954-1977* (1982) in Hamburger's and Walter Arndt's renderings and *Etchings & Words 1972-1982* (1985), which only contains translations by Hamburger. In April 1996 Harvest Books printed *Novemberland: Selected Poems 1956-1993*, its title deriving from a sequence of thirteen sonnets first published by *Agenda* in its 'German Poetry Special Issue' in summer 1994. It is noticeable that this bilingual volume which contains 54 poems was published in both a hardback and a paperback edition. In 1999 Faber & Faber, whose American headquarters are in Boston, published Grass's *Selected Poems 1956 to 1993*, with translations by Hamburger exclusively.

In addition to Grass, there are many German-language authors that Hamburger either first introduced to an American readership or whose American reception and reputation are considerably dependent on his translations. Among them are Albrecht Goes, Nelly Sachs, Adolf Muschg, Günter Eich, Hans Magnus Enzensberger, and Paul Celan. I will try to comment on the two authors last mentioned. Enzensberger, Hamburger recalls, most probably initiated the publication of the volume *Poems for People Who Don't Read Poems* by New York's

---

[12] Mueller, 'German Chronicle' 338.
[13] R.H.W. Dillard, rev. of *Shifts of Being*, by Richard Eberhart; *I'll Be Home Late Tonight*, by Thomas McAfee; *New Poems*, by Günter Grass, *The Kenyon Review* 31.3 (1969): 426-7. [425-7]

Atheneum Press in 1968, which contains translations by Hamburger, Jerome Rothenberg, and Enzensberger, and was also published in Great Britain by Secker & Warburg and Penguin the same year. According to Hamburger,

these translations should not have appeared in a single book, because the two languages – American and English – cannot be mixed. So that was really a mistake. At that time one could still just about get away with English translations in America, but nowadays people would just say, this is some foreign language. Even when the early translations of mine appeared in America, the eminent poet Kenneth Rexroth said in a review quite angrily, 'He uses these idioms which are British and do not mean anything to us.'[14]

The welcome this collection received from Michael Benedikt, as 'Critic of the Month' in *Poetry* (Chicago), was not warm at all; quite the opposite. Not only does he accuse Enzensberger of 'a weak style of political critique', 'slip[ing] from accurate, objective criticism into mere personal complaint', of 'massive rhetorical denunciations' and 'a general style of grievance'[15], but he also criticises Rothenberg's translations for misrepresenting the German poet by 'talking down':

The trap into which he has fallen is that of feeling he has to supply the German poet with the public touch, which he has further erred by identifying with the Common Touch. Three lines from a later section of 'Foam' are: 'o fire-eater with the heat turned off slip me some skin / o mummy in your mummy-cloth of pink-tinged foam god bless you / deliver your bubbling gullet to my kow-tow ...' Such phrases as 'slip me some skin', 'gullet', and 'kow-tow' are not suggested by the German original and are, to say the least, inappropriate. It is as if Enzensberger showed up to read some political poems in the United States wearing a zoot suit.[16]

If one reads the original alongside Rothenberg's translation, one easily recognises that the reviewer is wrong with regard to 'gullet'. Benedikt stresses, however, that Hamburger and Enzensberger avoid 'talking down'. Bloodaxe published *Selected Poems* in 1994 and *Kiosk* in early 1997, both of them being distributed in America by Dufour Editions in Chester Springs, Pennsylvania. Hamburger translated the majority of the poems published in Enzensberger's recent collections, to the latter the author added six translations of his own. The American author Lawrence Joseph, reviewing *Kiosk* for *Jacket* 4 (July 1998), an Internet quarterly edited by the Australian poet, John Tranter, stresses Enzensberger's exceptional 'vocal range

[14] Hamburger, personal interview.
[15] Michael Benedikt, 'The Shapes of Nature,' *Poetry* (Chicago) 113.3 (December 1968): 210. [188-215]
[16] Benedikt, 'The Shapes of Nature' 210-11.

and range of subjects' as well as two constants in his work: 'his preoccupation with how a poem sounds [...] and an acute, sophisticated sense of how these voices can be constructed in a poem. Often, a poem will switch, or seem to switch, speakers; we're in aesthetic realms similar to those of Gertrude Stein, Samuel Beckett, John Ashbery.'[17]

Paul Celan, whom Hamburger first met at Erich Fried's in London in 1952, was first introduced to a wider American readership by the inclusion of four poems – 'Fugue of Death' and 'The Jugs' in Middleton's renderings, 'Shibboleth' and 'In Memoriam Paul Éluard' translated by Hamburger – in the anthology *Modern German Poetry 1910-1960*. In 1971 it was again Dutton who took Celan's American reception history one – important – step further by publishing *Speech-Grille, and Selected Poems* in Joachim Neugroschel's rendering. In November 1972 Hamburger was awarded The Levinson Prize, which is presented annually by *Poetry* (Chicago), for his eleven translations of Celan (Dec. 1971) and the sections IV and V of *Travelling*, published in the magazine between October 1971 and September 1972. The next year the first important study in the field of American Celan-criticism appeared in Twayne's World Authors series, Jerry Glenn's 174-page book entitled *Paul Celan*. Persea Press in New York is the main outlet for Hamburger's Celan-translations. They published the bi-lingual collections *Poems* (bought from Carcanet) in 1980, *Poems of Paul Celan* (bought from Anvil Press) in 1989, and an enlarged and revised edition in 1994, but, as Hamburger stressed in the interview, they triggered hardly any response in America.

Hamburger's American reputation as editor and translator is usually associated with the publication of three mammoth bilingual anthologies: *Modern German Poetry 1910-1960* (with Middleton), *East German Poetry*, each being the first substantial collections of their sort to appear in America, and *German Poetry 1910-1975*. The reason that the first was published in 1962 by Grove Press, New York, was that Hamburger had already established a strong association with them. First of all, Hamburger contributed an essay to the inaugural issue of their magazine *Evergreen Review* in spring 1957, then they published his first book on German literature, *Reason and Energy* the same year, its revised edition entitled *Contraries* being issued by Dutton fourteen years later. For this anthology Hamburger and Middleton collected up what translations each had done, put them together and then decided that 'there were certain gaps and poets that neither of us had translated, but who ought to be in the book. Then we found other translators for those. We knew who was translating whom, since we both lived in London at that time and things were much more centralised than they are now.'[18] The anthology comprised 163 poems by 55 poets; in addition to the two editors, nine poets, among them Eva Hesse, Vernon Watkins, and David Luke, contributed twenty translations, which

---

[17] Lawrence Joseph, rev. of *Kiosk*, by Hans Magnus Enzensberger, *Jacket* 4 (July 1998) s.p. [http://www.jacket.zip.com.au/jacket04/joseph-enz.html]

[18] Hamburger, personal interview.

makes up only 12 per cent of the content. One third of the anthology is given over to poems by only six poets: Rainer Maria Rilke, Gottfried Benn, Georg Trakl, Georg Heym, Alfred Lichtenstein, and Bertolt Brecht. According to Hamburger, it sold pretty well both in America and in Great Britain where it had to be reprinted three times.

Many critics have misunderstood the creative relationship between Hamburger and Middleton. They first met in London in 1955 when Hamburger was teaching at University College and Middleton held a post as lecturer in German at King's College. They co-operated on various translation and editorial projects until 1966 when Middleton emigrated to America to take up the chair of Germanic languages and literature at the University of Texas, Austin. Many critics have thought that 'we translated together. We never translated together, we put together our translations. Even when I did a written interview a couple of weeks ago, I was asked to tell the interviewers about my supposed collaboration with Christopher Middleton over translation.'[19]

The only text Hamburger and Middleton ever collaborated on is the 24-page 'Introduction' to *Modern German Poetry 1910-1960*, which is a discussion of Expressionism and the modern style in German poetry initiated by it. They characterise the contents of the anthology by listing the poets omitted. They fall into six categories:

(1) those Naturalists, Impressionists and Symbolists whose work is either anchored in nineteenth century conventions, or not directly modern in style or outlook (e.g., Liliencron, Dehmel, George); (2) those poets whose work appeared well into this century but who were not affected by modernist techniques (e.g., Schröder, Borchardt, Carossa); (3) those poets who anticipated Expressionism in certain poems, but whose style or outlook is not central to it (e.g., Mombert, Dauthendey); [...] (4) poets of those bizarre, demi-prophetic, quasi-religious or otherwise quixotic groups which may be typical of the epoch but do not invariably claim attention as sources either of its best or even of its more charactered writing (e.g., Pannwitz, zur Linde, Derleth); [... (5)] those, like Elisabeth Langgässer or Nelly Sachs, whose work resisted translation,[20] and (6) with the exceptions of Brecht and Huchel, no East German poets are represented in the anthology, because, when we were choosing and translating poems, we had not read enough of their work to enable us to choose representative poems.[21]

---

[19] Hamburger, personal interview. This 54-page written interview Hamburger refers to was conducted by Peter Dale, former co-editor of *Agenda*, and published by *Between the Lines* in 1998.

[20] Michael Hamburger and Christopher Middleton, eds., 'Introduction,' *Modern German Poetry 1910-1960: An Anthology with Verse Translations* (London: MacGibbon & Kee, 1962) xxi.

[21] Hamburger and Middleton, eds., 'Introduction,' *Modern German Poetry 1910-1960* xlii.

Poetry (Chicago) published a review by David Galler, which is full of nationalist arrogance, implicit chauvinism, revenge, hatred, prejudice, and, perhaps, the sort of political correctness required at the time in some literary circles in America. Obviously, the gentleman had not read the anthology, but wanted to get rid of his anger bottled up over the years:

> Rilke, George, a few dozen poems by others, needed translating and received it. These 'others' – Trakl and Benn among them – were given a thorough treatment next; though many of their poems weren't worth it, one could accept the translators' love and effort. Hamburger and Middleton have overshot that mark with their anthology. What becomes painfully clear is the extent to which Hitler's régime stunted German poets of all ages, silencing many, truncating a tradition by forcing many to write secretly with no immediate masters and no means for public expression. The Germans, however, are a stubborn people; this anthology shows how, despite Hitler, most of them persisted right on through in writing poems with autotelic imagery enough to make one shudder. Small poetic progress in this country for over half a century![22]

With the next project, his bilingual *East German Poetry* anthology, which was begun under the auspices of the New York State Council for the Arts when Hamburger was visiting professor at State University of New York, Buffalo, in 1969 and finally published by Dutton Press in 1972, Hamburger tried to remedy one of the shortcomings of the first anthology. In this first major anthology of East German poetry to appear in the States, Hamburger collected 118 poems by twelve poets, with renderings by seven translators, among them Middleton, Ruth and Matthew Mead, and Christopher Levenson. Hamburger himself contributed more than half of the poems printed in the anthology, with the sections on Brecht, Heinz Kahlau, Reiner Kunze, Wolf Biermann, and Kurt Bartsch comprising translations done by Hamburger exclusively. In the 'Introduction' the editor stresses that 'it is not a representative anthology in terms of the political division, since that would have called for the inclusion of the sort of verse most in favour with the ideological directors of the régime

---

[22] David Galler, 'The Use of Anthologies,' rev. of *Tom Tiddler's Ground*, ed. Walter de la Mare; *The Crystal Cabinet*, ed. Horace Gregory and Marya Zaturenska; *Poet's Choice*, ed. Paul Engle and Joseph Langland; *Modern American Poetry* and *Modern British Poetry*, ed. Louis Untermeyer; *The Mentor Book of Major American Poets*, ed. Oscar Williams and Edwin Honig; *Modern German Poetry 1910-1960*, ed. Michael Hamburger and Christopher Middleton; *Modern Brazilian Poetry*, ed. John Nist, *Poetry* (Chicago) 103.4 (January 1964): 264. [261-5]

– exhortatory, self-congratulating pep-verse, antiquated even by the standards of the eighteen-nineties and subliterary in its complete subordination of the medium to the message.'[23] Among the criteria for inclusion Hamburger lists 'commitment to the truth of their own perceptions, feelings, and convictions', and a preoccupation 'with moral and social problems to a degree rare among non-communist poets', which, he thinks, 'is another reason why their work is, or should be, of special interest to American and British readers with no direct experience of an almost totally collectivized society.'[24] He would have liked to include work by Stefan Hermlin, Erich Arendt, and Peter Gosse, but their diction and verse forms 'proved too remote from the practice of their English-writing contemporaries.'[25]

Originally, this anthology was to be published first in America by a press in Buffalo – whose name Hamburger could not remember in the interview I conducted with him – but they let him down and nothing came of this. Then he sent it to Michael Schmidt, who accepted it and thereby started Hamburger's Carcanet career in Great Britain which lasted until the early 1990s when Hamburger broke with Schmidt, who – according to Hamburger – subsequently ordered all his books to be scrapped. Dutton, who had already published the revised edition of *Reason and Energy* as *Contraries* in 1971, took it over from Carcanet. In 1977 Carcanet published Hamburger's 500-page bi-lingual anthology *German Poetry 1910-1975*, whose co-publisher should have been Urizen Books, but it was finally withdrawn. According to Hamburger,

> there was a terrible disaster of the American edition. It first went to the translator Michael Roloff of Urizen Books, who was an eminent businessman on the New York publishing scene. They must have set it separately, because obviously the Carcanet edition was all right. I remember that I corrected the proofs, but then the book came out in his form and not in mine. It was withdrawn and the man disappeared from the publishing scene. Years later I got a summons to New York to go to a bankrupt proceedings. I was supposed to claim money from him for compensation for the damage, but I did not go and I just let it go.[26]

Inter Nationes in Bonn bought 3,000 copies for worldwide distribution, which enabled Schmidt to reprint it. In 1981 Schmidt sold the anthology to Persea Press in New York.

Although Hamburger compiled work by 95 poets in the anthology, he stresses

[23] Michael Hamburger, ed., 'Introduction,' *East German Poetry* (Oxford: Carcanet, 1972) xv.
[24] Hamburger, 'Introduction,' *East German Poetry* xv.
[25] Hamburger, 'Introduction,' *East German Poetry* xvi.
[26] Hamburger, personal interview.

that 'the contents of the anthology do not represent the whole of German, Austrian, and Swiss poetry written over a period of sixty-five years.'[27] However, it contains 'good and remarkable poems of as many kinds as I could respond to as a translator.'[28] Hamburger asked Middleton whether he wanted to collaborate again, but he turned down the offer: 'The reason is that by that time we were much more aware of how different the two of us were.'[29] According to Hamburger, the anthology 'sprang out of two needs: to collect scattered translations done over the decades and to replace the earlier anthology *Modern German Poetry 1910-1960*,'[30] which had been both out of print and out of date for some years. In 1978 Hamburger was awarded the Schlegel-Tieck prize for *German Poetry 1910-1975*.

The publicity campaign for this anthology received additional impetus by Hamburger's guest-co-editorship for *TriQuarterly* 35.2 (Winter 1976), which contains sections dedicated to German (ed. M. Hamburger), American (ed. Michael Anania), and French poetry (ed. Paul Auster). Hamburger was asked by the magazine's editor Elliott Anderson to select work from his – then – forthcoming anthology; the final selection, however, was done by Anderson himself, who printed 27 poems by 16 poets, such as Peter Handke, Günter Kunert, Reiner Kunze, and Jörg Steiner.

Hamburger the Critic

The widespread ignorance of literatures in German that Hamburger referred to when characterising the British (non-)reading public in the 1940s and 1950s – in his talk entitled 'The translator as an intermediary between two cultures' that was given in Amsterdam in March 1993 at the Foundation for the Production and Translation of Dutch Literature – holds true for today's situation in America:

> As for mediation, I could not rely on translations alone even with German-language writers as securely established in their own cultures now as Goethe, Hölderlin or Büchner. When my work began, in the 1940s, not only was there a strong prejudice against all things German in Britain, but an ignorance that extended to the most well-educated and sophisticated circles.[31]

Hamburger took the offensive by initiating an educational crusade by way of

[27] Michael Hamburger, ed. and trans., 'Introduction,' *German Poetry 1910-1975* (Manchester: Carcanet, 1977) xxxii-xxxiii.
[28] Hamburger, 'Introduction,' *German Poetry 1910-1975* xxxiii.
[29] Hamburger, personal interview.
[30] Hamburger, 'Introduction,' *German Poetry 1910-1975* xxv.
[31] Michael Hamburger, 'The translator as an intermediary between two cultures,' *PN Review* 92 (July-August 1993) 10. [9-10]
[32] Hamburger, 'The translator ...' 10.

complementing all his translations with 'critical writings, books of essays and obligatory introductions to the works and authors I translated.'[32] Ruth Klüger, painting the same dreary picture of the US reception of German literature in the early 1990s – in an essay published in a special volume of the influential German magazine *Text und Kritik* – holds that this ignorance has not been reduced a jot. If one asked Americans with an average education about twentieth-century German literature, they would most probably mention the names of Sigmund Freud and Franz Kafka. Intellectuals of the 1960s' generation might even know Thomas Mann's and Hermann Hesse's novels. Some may even have read Günter Grass's *The Tin Drum*. In her opinion, only small côteries in New York appreciate Peter Handke's and Thomas Bernhard's works, whereas US feminists are quite keen on Christa Wolf. According to Klüger, Rilke's poetry is widely known and appreciated.[33]

Against this context we have to appreciate the invaluable service that two US presses – Harcourt, Brace & World and Dutton – performed by publishing Hamburger's critical books *The Truth of Poetry: Tensions in Modern Poetry from Baudelaire to the 1960s* (1970) and *Contraries: Studies in German Literature* (1971) respectively. The latter is the revised edition of *Reason and Energy*, which appeared from Grove Press in 1957. At the same time, i.e., in 1970, Princeton University Press issued *Hofmannsthal: Three Essays*, which basically consists of Hamburger's introductions to the two volumes he edited for the Bollingen Foundation. Out of these three critical studies, *The Truth of Poetry* – where Hamburger provides his readers with a panorama of American and European poetry allocating German poetry its appropriate place – 'had most impact and is the only one that is still in print again, having been out of print for a long time.'[34] M.L. Rosenthal in *Poetry* (Chicago) said of Michael Hamburger's *The Truth of Poetry* that it is 'a richly concrete study', which

> is as intelligent a reconsideration of what has happened as one can find. [...] It is most useful in its overview of contemporary developments in Europe of some of the chief theoretical emphases of our day, all without arbitrariness if not without conviction, and is just one more sign of the awakening in the past few years of British criticism to the question of redefining 'modernity'. Apart from Hamburger's great specificity, I particularly like his understanding of the real, but protean, elusive, ever shifting and disappearing and reappearing connection between the mind's search for knowledge and practical wisdom and its entrancement by imagination, by

[33] Cf. Ruth Klüger, 'Zur Rezeption der deutschen Literatur im 20. Jahrhundert in den USA [The Reception of 20th Century German Literature in the United States],' *Text und Kritik* (special volume IX/1995: Ansichten und Auskünfte zur deutschen Literatur nach 1945) 132-35.

[34] Hamburger, personal interview.

aesthetic disinterestedness, and by the plastic possibilities of language.[35]

Hamburger started a second US crusade in the mid-1980s with the publication of *A Proliferation of Prophets: Essays on German Writers from Nietzsche to Brecht* and *After the Second Flood: Essays on Post-War German Literature*. 'The prose books were my attempt to bring into print all of Michael's durable essays in a kind of "collected" edition,'[36] Michael Schmidt of Carcanet Press told me by e-mail. St. Martin's Press, New York, was not Carcanet's co-publisher, but 'simply bought in 400-750 copies of our editions.'[37] However, they did not seem to go down well with the American reading public. Hamburger holds that 'they did not sell at all. [...] Somebody I know in America tried to buy one of those books. He could not get it from a bookshop. They were a complete flop.'[38]

Hamburger's role as critic is not restricted to the publishing of books. Between the mid-1950s and the early 1980s he also played an active role on the American little magazine scene as reviewer for prominent magazines, *Chicago Review* and *Poetry* (Chicago) among them. An excellent example of Hamburger the reviewer is his early review-essay on Erich Heller's *The Disinherited Mind: Essays in Modern Literature and Thought*, which was published in *Chicago Review* in spring 1958. The following extract is a good example of Hamburger's seriousness of approach to literature:

> [Professor Heller's criticism] expresses a discomfort which many have felt, but few have dared to voice. Though personally I am in favour of what Professor Heller calls 'spiritual timidity' in dealing with a matter at once so momentous and so slippery as the theme of this book, it is something to have the courage of one's despair. My own reaction to so extreme a claim for the philosophical approach to literature happens to be a recoil in favour of poetry; but then I have long ceased to live by a gospel compiled out of quotations by my favourite poets; and I have never been able to regard art, or any human activity whatsoever, as unrelated to all other human activities.[39]

---

[35] M. L. Rosenthal, 'Plastic Possibilities,' rev. of *Tragedy & Comedy: Four Cubist Plays*, by Paul Goodman; *The Garbage Wars*, by Donald Finkel; *Testament for My Students*, by Kay Boyle; *Lies*, by C.K. Williams; *Fifty Poems Fifty*, by Reed Whittemore; *A Quick Graph: Collected Notes and Essays*, by Robert Creeley; *The Truth of Poetry: Tensions in Modern Poetry from Baudelaire to the Nineteen-Sixties*, by Michael Hamburger, *Poetry* (Chicago) 119 (Nov. 1971) 103-104. [99-104]

[36] pnr@carcanet.u-net.com, 16.04.1998.

[37] pnr@carcanet.u-net.com, 16.04.1998.

[38] Hamburger, personal interview.

[39] Michael Hamburger, 'Of Truth Instead of Beauty,' rev. of *The Disinherited Mind: Essays in Modern Literature and Thought*, by Erich Heller, *Chicago Review* 12.1 (Spring 1958) 80. [74-80]

Another interesting example is his well-argued review-essay on David Young's translation of Rilke's *Duino Elegies*, which at the time of its publication was acclaimed by several prominent poets as *the* American rendering of Rilke's text, because Young's approach to translation – an attempt to make the text more contemporary, more American by breaking up Rilke's lines in the manner of William Carlos Williams's 'variable foot' – runs counter to Hamburger's ethos:

> If it were really necessary for literary works, even works as recent, relatively speaking, as the *Duino Elegies*, to be thoroughly modernized, 'updated', in every regard whenever they are newly translated, the implication would be that a contemporary work in English, *The Waste Land*, for instance, calls for similar treatment if it is to remain 'alive' and 'urgent'. This makes the assumption not only false but insulting, since it would mean that readers have become incapable of the slightest effort of adjustment to conventions and periods other than their own. That there are such readers, that there is a trend that way – even among professors who have ceased to believe in what they profess – leaves no doubt as to where that assumption leads.[40]

Instead of a Resumé

Finally, some comments on the title of my essay: the reason why I would like to describe Hamburger's translations as 'celebration of German literature' is connected with his ethos, which he sums up at the end of his 'Introduction' to *German Poetry 1910-1975*, when he says: 'Like all my translations, these take no more liberties than are needed to come as close as possible to the original texts, that is their tone, gesture, tension, dynamic of feeling as much as their surface "meaning". My hope is that they will convey something of the quiddity of each poem, not of my quiddity [...].'[41]

Hamburger's influence as translator of German literature is adequately summed up by the British poet Rodney Pybus in a judgment which, I believe, also holds true for many American readers: 'Everyone who has been reading poetry in English in recent decades (especially those without German) is in Michael's debt, for opening so many windows into German literary culture.'[42]

---

[40] Michael Hamburger, 'Music and Meaning', rev. of *Duino Elegies*, by Rainer Maria Rilke, trans. David Young, *Poetry* (Chicago) 134 (July 1979) 236. [234-40]

[41] Hamburger, 'Introduction', *German Poetry 1910-1975* xxxiii.

[42] Rodney Pybus, 'Growing Apples at 70: A Tribute to Michael Hamburger', *Stand Magazine* 35.2 (Spring 1994) 5. [4-5]

Andrew Waterman

Happiness

for my son Rory on his wedding

Remember that day at Yarmouth?
I watched the cone in your grip
tilting, until *splat!*
on the pavement, your world
lost… But the man in the shop
gave you another ice-cream, free.
The seaside came back.

The next year, happiness
was a tree-house, high and dry
among greenery filtering
sunlight and bird-song,
a ladder up to it and
the steel pole to slide down
to the little train that circuited
the grounds, past water.

Then came the paper boats
we folded to race on the Witham,
more fragile vessels, some
were pecked ragged by swans.

All these were a long time ago
– longer for you than for me;
that is the way time goes,
contracting as we pass it.
Teaching us loss
that knows no remedy,
settings-out that never
come round full-circle,
and how soon, as for those boats,
dissolution comes
in the shrugging welter.
And also this:
that the truest happiness
is when life finds some use for
the love we ache to give.

We cannot command it. Choosing
(as we must) may betray us.
Or, suddenly dancing
like snowflakes under a streetlamp,
it melts at the touch of earth.

Denied it, all we achieve
means only ashes,
the scald of tears.

All we can do is be ready.

Diana Brodie

Wedding Music

After the wedding guests had gone,
my daughter, curls tumbling,
golden skirt flying,
was dancing with your son
to music of their making
which you interpreted
as a waltz and we danced too.

Next morning when I thought
you had already gone,
it made me jump to see
you back in the kitchen doorway.
Silent. Hesitant.
Silhouette with briefcase.
Magritte's man without his bowler hat.
Somewhere, distant music played
but with a change of key.

Papers laid across the table,
you read from their thin vocabulary.
    In phrasing staccato.
Born in Vilnius.
Murdered in Dachau.
    Basso ostinato.

Died in Auschwitz.

basso ostinato: 'a short bass phrase repeated many times with varied upper parts'.
                              (The Concise Oxford Dictionary of Music)

Glass Heads

In the shaping, while it's still hot, the glass is at
its most beautiful, a potent mix of spirit, wind and fire.
Old Roubíček the glass sculptor breathes himself
into an almost-man-sized blowpipe; when that

is done, he deftly pulls, presses, punches, cuts,
entwines and spins. This, he says, *is all adventure*
and until the flame has died, the glass has cooled,
who knows what will happen next? Because

each alteration in the breath, slight turn of hand,
a surge or loss of faith, can alter everything.
The sculptor longs to make the glass as beautiful cold
as when it's hot, to keep it singing, in joy or in lament.

In an upper room of a Prague museum is Roubíček's
lifetime's work. A colloquy of glass heads crowds together
on the plinth; some incline, one to another, wind-
whispering trees in a featureless forest of Bohemia.

These heads have no eyes to see or mouth to speak.
Of their identities, few clues remain:
upon one head some added twists of golden glass
are all that's left of curls which trailed

once to a curving nape of neck. Most heads are smooth,
bowed, shaven and reduced. Not far from here,
the camp at Terezín, known as Paradise Ghetto,

was full of music, played in secret attics
on smuggled instruments. Terezín's 'Ghetto Swingers'
kept up their playing until the end, while Bach's Chaconne,

they say, *helped overcome hunger* and the playing
drowned the crack of early morning gunfire
from the nearby Rumbuli forest.

Nigel Jarrett

Nuptials

A photo came to me
of my parents' wedding,
a wartime union with much
forced jollity cancelled
by 'damn-the-Hun' sentiment
(my grandmother, hand on hip
and wearing a floral utility frock
with cocked straw hat), yet
notable for the Dégas-like
composition of a snapper trying
to be formal with a tripod,
and sending – Oh, sod it! -
a strange image down the years
of my father and mother pictured
with a random uncle and aunt,
who are gazing at something out of shot
and not noticing my old man's
pained features, as though even then
he was snagged by the guts-ache
that would double him daily
till he died sixty years later
of something unrelated for which
he had no cupboard stash of pills
(his suffering mirror image
opening on to its patent relief),
and I'm thinking that this ready-made
expression was for every time I hurt him,
as though I was bound to let him down,
and that here he is still willing me
to prove that I could go one better
and be what he couldn't, beguiled
by the light that brings just
another day, temperate save for dreaming.

Warrior

You never went to war, *mein Vater,* caught you packet deep
In that grease monkeys' temple, grimacing by caged lamplight
Under trucks revving for battle, those doomed platoons queuing
For your rack-stretched anthems. Where was it they sent you –
A Craiglockhart for non-combs (exponents of the twenty-hour day,
Plodders frozen by the mystery of no longer wanting to cope)?

And your collier father before, hacking out a deeper burrow
Than all his mates had at Vimy Ridge, tame, pick-triggered sparks
Mimicking the icy starburst they wrote home to Sis about
In the fingerless mittens she'd made. He found stillwater silence, too;
Lived on, their keen progenitor, to learn of Watson and Crick,
Fates spiralled in helices. And here I am now, waiting
For news from another front beside this bed in this monument
To bright dew and bloody sweat. (Is that why we fought two wars?
Friends asked, watching a TV 'suit' slither 'twixt title and privilege.)
Surgeons stitch chests *sans* lungs – redoubt held for another day –
But they'll soon be back at base to say your wounds are fatal.
You knew all along, of course: the surnamed bullet, and all that.

I see only your pillowed head, guess at the tucked-in rest of you,
Racing madly beyond the end, and I wonder if the dark's for me,
Whose life is mere skirmishing, will choose me for the Fallen
Who has lived to mourn the numberless and, with time others bought,
Watched the housemartins – *Hirundines* – wheeling in again,
Mercury fled from Mars, the cycle advanced, but a cycle.

Dylan Willoughby

What Blossoms

When you breathed, it was as if you had kissed flame
You paced, the tube dragging along the floor
Attached to your nose, a cannula, 'little reed'
That took its breaths for you, its music
Not the spring song you had once hummed
Nor the *mon coeur* of Saint-Saëns you sang
When voice and heart awoke at Juilliard
In a budding spring that never brought flower

A month's old Opera News half-read, its mouth
Open on your nightstand, as if everything
Might break into song, the old Callas records
Rise up and play themselves on the old LP,
Scratchy but otherworldly all the same
Even now you try to sing

Be no sleeper in the dust, eschew any silent
Abodes, blow down the muted gates of *sheol*!
If they have no Porgy and Bess, protest
And think of us . . .

You died today. Driving home, the radio played
Mahler's *Blumine*, his discarded blossoms
So beautiful they brought rain,
This late bouquet . . .

Old Growth

(At Muir Woods)

Fogs ghost the ancient redwoods
In this Cathedral Grove
The fallen carcass the floor
Where sword ferns cut through
Toyon berries sprout red
There the burnt snag leans
A wooden cairn, an obelisk
Saplings root into its death
As the shades lavish occult rain

Greg Delanty

At My Mother's Bed

(Marymount Hospice, Cork)

Tonight I keep watch over you dying,
the most peaceful night I ever knew.
I suppose it's the release of your going
drawn out over chemo months into
years. I soothe your agitated hand. You lie
under the nimbus of the nightlight, reflected in
the black window—your bed and you fly
in the pane above the city's Saturday-night din.
Pure Chagall. You head into the stars,
over Summerhill, Capwell, Evergreen, the Black Ash;
hover above familiar streets and lanes, above bars
folk sing in. There is no need to dash.
Your name has just been noble-called.
Sing *South of the Border* one last time. You
raise your voice above the Lee, the town you hauled
a lifetime of plastic bags through,
bowing into the drizzle, drudging home
over North Gate Bridge, up Blarney Lane;
our city of hills, our 'Frisco, our Rome,
our Buenos Aires, our Varanasi. It starts to rain.
Your hand must be waving adios. Ma,
the night sky reflects our city below.
Now every light's a votive candle, your Fatima.
Behold the glass darkly. There you go.

Note. 'Noble Call' is a term used in Cork City for the custom that gives the singer at a sing-along the right to choose the next person to sing.

A Small Prayer

Something I can't put a finger on is slotting back into
      place, something that's had me imbibe
my way through parties, seek indiscriminate company,
      talk too much. It's time to be myself again,
to swab what is called spirit with the balm of solitude.
      The ointment of silence is accentuated by the sound
of the sea, the cuckoo, the moorhens at night, a cock
      from Fitzgerald's barn crowing every few minutes
there's still time. The silence of a midday empty chapel
      an unnoticed pensioner has dropped into
to thank God for some small prayer answered.

Geraldine Paine

The unmarked grave

Twisting two ribboned plaits, a child
waits by a woman

in a scullery with a deep sink; tries
to follow as the curtain rises.

Why put old heads on young shoulders,
she'll wear white gloves every day!

She hears little off-stage, the doors close
on whispers. But this is her play

where sudden death has no part
and ration books are shared

with flying visitors
in the London flat still standing.

She watches from the wings
as the fine crumbs fall –

the start of the *Mamie*
and Nan Routine!

One day, she'll use the scalloped bowl,
the rolling pin, the jug,

for treacle tarts, Cornish pasties,
the light and bright star-gazey pies.

and pass on praise
instead of flowers.

Anne Ryland

My Mother's Salt Coat

It was no longer possible to glimpse
over her shoulder; there was grinding-forward only.
The lining gritted her skin.

But the salt coat kept her upright,
sheltered her from windlash.
She was carrying all her grandmothers on her back.

She'd imagine handfuls of berries dropping
into the pockets – then they'd burst,
shedding redness down the coat,

the stain turning the road ahead of her
the same colour the world was
from behind closed eyelids.

At dusk the coat crust was a snow-blue white,
icing her for the winter.
Yet she had disobeyed no-one.

The buttons were salt crystals still growing;
at night they glinted
until thieves followed her

and she almost longed to be robbed of this greatcoat.
The taste of it thirsted her out,
the swallowing and swallowing

as lost dogs licked her into a pillar.
Her pulse stuttered, the silence was soft –
she was locked inside the monument of her body.

Wendy Robinson

Autolycus: Old Crow

Prelude

Autolycus, Old Crow:
Prompt – Fridays –
Platform 5, 7.25 –
Each time, for months,
I caught the 7.35 –
Because my sister was dying:

To the North

You flap in – ancient,
Slightly crazed landing
Like an Old Lancaster.
You set about it –
Life –
Head thrusting back and forth,
Back and forth –
To persuade your body
To come along with you –
Me too:
The weight of Things –
A heavy rocking
Of grief not birth.

Not much on offer –
We both pecked
For crumbs of comfort –
Autolycus, Old Crow,
Carrion comfort,
Comfort in woe.

Weakly, weekly, I wanted to bring you –
Extras.
But it wouldn't do.
Death and scarcity have to be lived –
Some – how?

Postlude

Months later:
Not your time –
Not your platform,
I took the 10.45 to London –
You flapped in awkwardly –
Landing within an inch of my foot.
You may be a snapper-up
Of ill-considered trifles,
But you know how it is,
Between this world and the next –
Autolycus, Old Crow.

       Autolycus, Old Crow,
       Crow come lately,
       Crow come soon –
       Never come never –
       Crow come.

Erinn Batykefer

Cicada Year

It made sense when the cicadas, bottle-green
and shining, dug themselves into the air and shook
years of dirt from their glazed wings. I had seen
their lacquered curves under glass, in a nook
of the museum's Egypt wing: polished scarabs lined
up like lozenges, the glittering insects of archaeology.
Here they were, in the backyard, living second lives
like pharaohs risen from dirt to drone in the trees,
shedding their skins like burial linen. I followed the creek's
Nile-bright scribble into the woods and found their shells
clinging to sycamores and the white undersides of leaves.
I read the pinprick hieroglyphs etched on peeling bark like scrolls,
And when my pale skin split like a shell and I rose through
Childhood's long sleep, I knew my cicada life. This turning into.

Apple Family

Georgia O'Keefe, c1920

Clean linen and the apples pierced to pomanders,
the window-lights' reddish haloes like the soft darkness
inside bodies, behind eyelids –

all the white silver and dinner plates
clicking like the minute en masse movement
of blood cells percolating,

the frisson of saline charged with motion –
I've seen this color before. Another red-letter day,
Winter, 1982. Between us, a whisper

moving on iambs of blood: *it's time it's time.*
Beyond the frost-sprigged windows and wreathed doors,
there is bone-cracking cold,

the body's sudden, unlicked edges.
I remember my inconsolable mouth without teeth.
I remember being unable to speak,

the livid frustration of things known –
the apples lined up just so, red against white –
of things known but impossible to tell.

Alex Smith

Hortyard

In celebration of Rivers Nursery Orchard, Sawbridgeworth, Hertfordshire

i

The Nectaren, and curious Peach ...

Order -
Marvell, Hobbema, a man
attending fruit trees

patient, twine held
between thumb,
forefinger and teeth

his shovel hat
protective against
the broken northern sky.

His innocence is stern, profound.
Unknowing, he twists the stems
and twines of empire:

gardener, builder, accountant,
factotum, moralist:
he's what this country's made of.

ii

Vines and branches trained,
constrained. The fruit will fall
when ripe, in God's good time

and not before. Like his daughters
he observes, subject to control
beneath the claims of nature.

He snatches off his hat
in harvest-reverence, kneeling
with heartfelt thanks –

Esther and Ruth there,
nudging and winking
in the pews.

iii

Nocturnal

Observe now the Lappet,
Herald and Clifden Nonpareil
clinging to sugared bark.

That sticky ooze is all
as they converge in a cloaked mass
of camouflage. Fruit swells

to porcelain gloss
in moonlight. A beetle
stumbles through jungled grass.

Armoured and horned,
swivel-eyed, they emerge
from your bad dreams, tuck

into the folds
of the discarded blanket.
                    The orchard
hunkers, streaked in pewter light.

iv

Another part of the wood

Sambre, Marne, Oise, Somme ...
the nightmare landscape
of blasted, skeletal trees.

Hell's orchards, draining like a sump
into history. Even crows
abandon this moon-terrain:

end of the human spoor,
end of the feral road,
of any road.

v

I have seen Eden

A return to the fulness thereof.
Not the swagger of Augustus
on the Palatine, spitting pips,

or patrician casualness,
thick voiced among squander,
but an order of care,

taciturn, only too conscious
of what we are. *What thou thyself
hatest, do to no man* –

have we kept with that?
Well then, respect reserve
in others. Bind the twines

and cultivate – Thomas Rivers,
Conference, Fertility,
Curlew and Stint. Name the fruits

as Adam named them, granting
cadences of order
to a world of encounter.

References:

The title 'Hortyard' is one of the old spellings of 'orchard'.
The Nectaren, and curious Peach – 'The Garden', Andrew Marvell (1621-78).
Meyndert Hobbema, Dutch painter (1638-1709).
Lappet, Herald and Clifden Nonpareil are moths, all active at night.
I have seen Eden – The opening of 'Eden', a poem by Charles Tomlinson.
'The fulness thereof' – from the opening of Psalm 24.
What thou thyself hatest, do to no man – Jewish wisdom from the Talmud.
'Thomas Rivers', 'Conference', 'Fertility', 'Curlew' and 'Stint' – all names of fruit produced by Thomas
Rivers & Son, Sawbrdigeworth. The first is an apple; 'Conference' and 'Fertility' are pears; 'Curlew'
and 'Stint' are plums.

Charlie Parker in Saffron Walden

No longer to feel the continual oppression
and narrowness of others' vision
but to stride, lung-full, across
our wind-gust English common
noting dogs and children
in their playful heedlessness.

And perhaps you would manage
such an abrupt shock of change
by making a dramatic entrance,
announcing your presence
with a liquid spill of notes
like a clear stream skipping over
its bed of varicoloured stones,
sweeping us along with
What is this thing called love.

Roger Elkin

Water Barrel

Ribbed zinc tub, rough to touch,
mid-fifties washday relic, it was propped
on bricks at the greenhouse end.

Its comfortable rotundity seemed out of place
against the angled glass. Dad's rectangular beds,
straight lines, his patterned planting out, row
after tidy row, file on file.

Coldly factual, he calculated it in gallons,
measured out how long before he needed
to keep the rainwater topped up
so there'd always be enough for me
to bucket-lug and slush round his dahlia canes.

I yenned to own its seasonal wealths:
those arteries of ice hanging down
its January sides; the Spring meniscus
of its eye filled with clouds and sky;
and, especially after May, its living world
of flick-flacking 'things' jigging at its rim.

Wondering what they were, I'd up-
end the butt and watch that water
with its rivery-stink bowling down the path
in deltas of slurry. There was grit enough
and sand and grime the sum of months,
but never ever 'things'.

Dad roaring at this *Waste of water*
restored the tub upright, its emptiness
thwanging in the clang of zinc
and him demanding Why? Why? Why?

*

Decades later, the summer air
a haze of dancing gnats,
I have the answer to his question

but know he never guessed
just how those barrelled depths
measured out our separateness.

103

Chrys Salt

Lost

(March 2003)

There are no maps for poets in this country.
The compass finger, mindless on its post
will not direct us on this dangerous journey.
An unfamiliar landscape tells us we are lost.
Above the bramble and the rambling wood
the wheeling dragons search for bones
of luckless travellers who have misconstrued
the alien symbols on the milestones.
We have nowhere to go but where we are,
our options closed, the exit double locked.
We may not take direction from a star.
The stars are out and all the roads are blocked.
How can we dare this nightmare territory?
The shifting contours of the hills and coasts,
the gibberish signposts and the season's enmity.
What hand our touchstone in this land of ghosts?

John White

Tullanee

I swung the rented motor grass-wards out
of harm's way pondering how the name
they'd christened it in ancient days still suited
the old place, *hill of the raven*,
that snarl of wind and twigs and blackened roots.

They fed the vexed Elijah bread and meat,
this lumpen crowd of outsize choughs
each squat and plumed in Calvinistic gown
above that barn now dignified to *chorch*,
the thorn that's left after the rose has gone.

The skyline's sometimes haze, more often mist.
Today the creeping Foyle's so distant
it's congealed, like you could walk to Inishowen
and back, drop in to catch a singsong
in Moville and hardly wet your feet.

Midway up the slope the weather turns.
Rain runs across my back burning like ice
from off the trees and onto headstones
(*Let not your heart be troubled* my father's text)
forever overlooking and overlooked.

It stops and all you catch is the still small voice
of a dripping tap on hand for you to water
flowers either clouding under glass
like breathing eyes or wetter than a trifle
beneath branches stiff as tuning forks

that once had stoked the stumbling faithful,
one of whom nods back to me – it's better left
unsaid, this slippery path, the whispering air
about our heads, birds fidgeting in nests
become enormous year by year.

John Powell Ward

Love

Some name it affection.
A discharge of
Loganberries drifts in
From the poem itself.

Does heaven exist,
They demand? Very mind is heaven.
The soul's deaf-and-dumb
Windmills queenly

In the toxic reeds, blamed
At matins for their
Jangling street-cars' hues
Of cobalt and tan.

As planetary countrymen
You fear, and you fear,
Our verbal specifics.
Our crazed mileage.

Attending the coup of
These sage twilights,
My dream's hairdresser,
Whose very bone melts down.

Susan Minish

Voyaging

We buried her today.
No! That is not it:
We just folded away her coat,
Put it reverently in its box.

In truth, we drew in her mooring lines,
All the tugs and tenders
Had inched her out from the rough sea wall;
She was already under way.

She seems connected still,
But she is heading for open water,
Her canvas rattling up her mast.
Set on the timeless voyage.

For a long time we will see
Her sails in our spyglass,
Bright-work shining in the sun
And her own flag crackling
In a wind we cannot hear.

Brendan McMahon

Owls

The owl on the roof has flown unimaginable distances
to bring us this song it has learned from the dead;
it is stone, it is empty, it's here and it's gone
and we do not want to hear it, huddling feebly
to avoid the high, cold eyes of dawn.

Song

The candle's flamedance, you have that
accuracy and grace. You are
the looked-for ghost in your loved,
forgotten place, a wordless,
tuneless song. Your footsteps in the dust
of morning are imperceptible
as the shadow of a star.

Three things are hard to catch:
love, the silver flash of May,
and your evasive heart.

Chris Jones

Nevermas

Never to Naxos
  Or home to a woman waiting
    in white linen and lipstick,
      pouting at the pretty Greek boys
and singing jazz in a cracked voice,
    out-of-key and dusky with nicotine
Never a landing.

Never such wakeful nights
    reading poems to the dawn
Never the dew renewed.

Never you and the broken bowl of a lute
    thrumming with the struck gut-strings
run taut
    and stoking the bowl with song
Never Aramaic
  or ancient Hebrew vowels
                        on her tongue
Nor the heart in its dish, saved from ovens of clay
Or the palace of the Doges
              rising
  from the waves of twenty-eighth century Adriatic
Never *resurgam*.

Never the motif repeated
    to fashion pattern out of precedent,
  sewing the silver thread right
              through to the very

Never a communist bar in Berlin.

Never in secluded chapel,
  their bodies whispering mutual prayers
The cold cinder a smouldering coal.

Never an orchard's planting hole
    dug to the depth of a spade-spit

Majesty of
      unhunted deer herds
ghosting the ha-ha
      haunting the parkland

Procession of celebrants
  and guests dressed for banquet
The gods never spilling
                            through
           to fill the evening valley
                                  with a gentle infinite light

Never grief
      over autumn un-
                  folding her dominion
    of leaf
           and leaving

Never regret.

Never
      regret.

John Gibbens

A Yellow Rose

        which turns
the wrist of storms
and the sleeping metals
of a twilight,
fastened with no longer
bolt than fragrance
around the gentle wires
of zero's eye,
to cups, that absence may
last in the mind
more ringingly than bronze.

Dwelling

After ranging
a place in the mind like a marsh,
salt and sinking,
and scarcely green and grey,
under weathers as plain and harsh,
from that briny thinking,
from a changeless changing
tide's estranging
I turn away

to where you sleep
and come to rest alongside you.
Down to the ferns
of its floor, among leaves,
the sunlight of darkness slides through
that wood to which night turns,
thickets, where dread may creep
or hope's deer leap,
our breathing weaves.

Roland John

The Old Ironworks

When the wind's edge moves over grasses
I have heard them, the many memories
in these woods; fifteen years I've walked here,
passed the pot-bellied kilns hidden under roots,
noting where once the mill wheels screamed
amongst sweating men beating iron into tools.

For almost 200 years these valleys echoed
with their labour. I have seen the catalogues
of their productions, agricultural and domestic;
slashing bills, hooks and cucumber frames,
a vast industry powered by these gentle streams
once boxed in and dammed for their power.

Gone now and scarce a trace remains, a few
low walls, a pattern of rails in the grass,
scrub covered slag heaps, the occasional
implement, ironwork rusting back into earth;
a skeleton exposed of what once lived –
but listen; their voices still heard on the water.

The Collector

I wait on them that fear me most,
Heedless of age, caste, class or race,
I trawl the land and reap the coast
Never slipshod, a sure, measured pace
Assembling my party of guests plus host
And then I'm off without a trace.

My route is dark; I leave scarce a trace,
Perhaps a pattern in the air that most
Discount; yet some in the Elevation of the Host
Seek the deliverance of the race
As they pray, implore and pace
Seeking redemption on the phantom coast.

The blasted beach or tourist coast
Daily cleansed of grief, prints or trace
Is still my domain to wait and pace
Watching for those that haunt me most
Believing I'm of that fallen angelic race
Not knowing I'm only a febrile host,

Feeble perhaps but still that host
Who plies his way along their coast
Pursuing those that try to race
Ineffectually striving to remove all trace
Of what they once believed in most;
Now trapped they fall and lost the pace.

With ease I glide and soon outpace,
Ignoring their chalice and its host,
I am the one that yearns the most
Ready to tarry on that blighted coast
Without habitation, soon without trace
Of this bizarre and meretricious race.

They're snared wherever they race
Thinking their plodding pace
Can be a match for mine. I trace
Them in churches, upset their host
Defy their faith on every coast
This cult of liars I hate the most.

The last race is over for this host
Of fools that pace their dismal coast,
No trace of hope for these I fear the most.

Sue Roe

Drawing a Peach

I have slid my amber stones
one by one
out of the little hole in each lobe
he said he couldn't remember

they are tawny as his eyes
I miss their heaviness
they used to hang gravid, smooth
as a cupboard, a spoon, in each ear

this pencil lead's a femur
hard against its muscle of board
stepping back to look and look
I'm checking the stone

in the open peach, pulled
roughly apart, lying splayed
one half darkening against the other
bruised, dappled, dulled

watching for signs
of decay, its amber flesh
wearing away at itself
recoiling from the heart

the valves webbed against its hard nut
fibrous, granulated, bony
each side open as the sun moves round
pulped, wetter, as if bloody

when I step up close again
I miss the heavy swing
of my amber, warm as a split peach
smooth as a polished crater

The Artist's Wife as a Young Girl

unfurling after the rain
haughty, talkative, undone

hair down, tangles of green
brushed around her like a screen

brows and eyes set deep
young mouth creased

her starlet-face,
Marie, full of grace ...

but she twists, and in that shift
he saw the twists

of every living thing,
the power, the moving spring

life falling down
cascading down around

a dark wash of green,
flesh creaming

alive, sprung, diagonal
there where he saw it first

Hortense, eighteen,
the thing first seen

(after Cézanne : *Young Girl with Unbound Hair*)

Will Stone

Harrowing

Do you see the old moon waiting,
a tired gull tethered to the harrow
above the dawn reluctant field.
Do you see the rabid activists,
book brandishers, men of power
burning crude effigies for the crowd
and how even this evil is absorbed
by the eye blink of a deer in a glade?
Do you see the unblemished children
prodding the ditch with sticks?
They are finding out what it feels
to sink down an escalator in the mall
into the cutlasses of neon,
the vacancy encrusted men and women,
finery of the pit where coinage entrails
spill themselves unashamed.
Do you see this and weep for another age
which is only a mocking fantasy,
a tail pinned on the donkey,
a desperate raking of coals, brief glow,
piano played by the tramp's filthy nails,
or another rower whipped aboard
your heart's slow slave ship.
Feel the prow dip and drink,
only momentum and more funerals,
the warmth of child and mother
slipping away into jaundiced snow.

Kate Scott

All the men I've never slept with

gather in the room.
I run my fingers down their runner-bean spines
to their apple-tight buttocks, their courgette thighs.
Their skins are glistening: dark as aubergine,
pale as parsnip.
How they would dance:
Two-four, four-four, eight!
I count and count and count.

And then you get up;
the men scatter to the walls, rattled like dry rice.
Strolling past, you lay your hand upon my head,
brand me with your warmth.
And all the men I've never slept with
go passing through the chink in the door,
slip into the untasted night.

Linda Benninghoff

August

I can still feel your hands
as they closed around the can-opener
alongside mine, as we opened
together the can of mushroom soup.

A gray-blue catbird
ambled near the window
this cold August.
One day he threw himself
against a pane
again and again,
leaving a pale shape of wings
on the glass.

You left a memory
which I touch gingerly
with only the edges of my hands.

Daniel Tobin

The Late Show

The films reel on and won't wind back again.
That magic button on your VCR
fires blanks for the wrong cosmic station,
could ply dead letters from galactic blurs
whirling darkly beyond the room's reflection.
Here, pixels hum in economies of flight,
lifetimes figured on the screen's blue glare.
These shadows alive in flickers of light

move like musings in a mind's obsession—
This gaff, that fear, has made you who you are.
The plots nose by on their bounded ocean
of wrongs, regrets, and unresolved desires.
The stalker with his surly air, his passion
for revenge, almost trumps the family's plight.
The crook that dies alone, the ruthless star,
each shadow alive in its flicker of light,

each pair of haunted lovers, illusions
of loss or hope or want, pass by your stare
that in this *numen* would seem carved in stone
if you could watch yourself, night's voyeur
attending your own window's incarnation
of a square immersing the world in its sight.
It shines, you'd say, *it's awash and lunar,
my shadow alive in its flicker of light:*

The sun surrounds us but our eyes are tar.
That would be true if Plato were right
and the cave had a portal, and the mirror
lived, more than shadow, a flicker of light.

Obituary

W. S. Milne

Edward Lowbury, 1913-2007

Edward Lowbury, the distinguished bacteriologist (his parents had presciently named him Edward Joseph Lister Lowbury) and poet, who died last year at the age of 93, was a regular contributor to *Agenda* over the years, gracing the magazine with some of his finest poems.

Lowbury was born in London in 1913, a doctor's son, and was educated at St. Paul's School and at University College, Oxford, where he read medicine, completing his medical training at the Royal London Hospital just before the outbreak of the Second World War. Whilst at Oxford he won the Newdigate Prize for poetry in 1934, and the Matthew Arnold Memorial prize in 1935. His first book of verse, *Port Meadow*, was published in 1936. His war service was spent mainly in Kenya with the Royal Army Medical Corps, with a period of fire-watching through the Blitz. After the war Lowbury worked in the Common Cold Research Unit before his appointment to the Birmingham Accident Hospital where for thirty years he was head of the microbiology department at the Medical Research Council burns unit. Whilst there he wrote some 200 papers on topics such as the behaviour of bacteria in burns and wounds, on disinfection, and on antibiotic resistance (a topic of particular relevance in today's hospitals), travelling widely in the USA and contributing to reports on hospital infection. His influential handbook *The Control of Hospital Infection* (1975), as *The Guardian* obituary said, commands more sales than most volumes of contemporary poetry!

Lowbury said that it was meeting poets associated with Yeats' friend T. Sturge Moore in Hampstead that first inspired him to write, but at the same time acknowledged that 'medicine was probably a better background than a wider knowledge of literature for writing about life, which I took to be an essential function of poetry', an idea embodied in his poem about fire-watching, for instance, where he writes 'it's the animal in you that insists on life.' The same feeling is there in his poems about Africa – about huntsmen felling gazelles and lions in the Mua Hills.

A friendship with the pastor-poet Andrew Young led to Lowbury marrying Young's daughter, Alison, who later, with her husband, wrote a candid biography of her father (published in 1997). Edward and Alison also edited together a *Selected Poems of Andrew Young* for Carcanet Press in 1998. The novelist David Lodge was encouraged to write by Lowbury whilst working in Birmingham. Lowbury took a keen interest in the topic of doctor-poets (naturally enough), and he and his wife wrote a biography in 1970 of Thomas Campion concentrating on the inter-relationship between medical care and care for the word.

He had no time for the C.P. Snow 'Two Cultures Debate', arguing for both sides of the coin, that 'old myths may still move us more than new knowledge', delighting in the fact that Brückner found the opening of his Seventh Symphony in a dream as August Kekulé did the structure of the benzene molecule.

Perhaps Lowbury's best known volumes of poetry are *Time for Sale* (1961), *Daylight Astronomy* (1968), and his work for children *Green Magic* (1972), and perhaps his most powerful poem is the one he wrote the day after the atom bomb was dropped on Nagasaki, first published in *Equator*, the magazine of the Mombasa Arts Club:

August 10th, 1945 – The Day After

Who will be next to break this terrible silence,
While the doom of war still shivers over these
Unwilling either to die or to be defeated, –
In the agony of death still torn, contorted,
Torn between saving face and body, both
Mutilated almost beyond recognition?
The face fights on long after
The body's overwhelmed and hacked to pieces.
Every scar of it's their fault; yet I am dumb;
In the blind eyes of pity the good and the evil
Are equals when they're gasping in the sand,
Helpless. The reality so blinds
Our senses that it seems less than a dream,
Yet we shall live to say 'Twice in a lifetime
We saw such nakedness that shame
Itself could not look on, and of all the feelings,
Hate, anger, justice, vengeance, violence, –
Horror alone remained, its organ voice
Searching us with a sickening clarity.'
And now the word comes in of those two cities
With all their living burden
Blown to the wind by power
Unused except by God at the creation, –
Atomised in the flash of an eye.
Who else but God or the instrument of God
Has power to pass such sentence?
Here the road forks, to survival or extinction,
And I hold my tongue through the awful silence,
For if God had nothing to do with it,
Extinction is the least price man can pay.

Rarely do the talents of the man of science and the man of arts meet so harmoniously and so intelligently in one person as they did in Edward Lowbury. *Agenda* has lost a much treasured, and a very cultured, friend.

John Kinsella

Requiem

Anniversaries defoliate maps.

Remember where you've come from
and the general fixedness of celestial bodies: flaw
therein worth a life-change
or realigning

as purpose is to accolades,
ministries to choirs

mosquitoes thicker
near the river
conserved
so join up
to make little difference, thwarting
mortgage-ocracies, national corporatism
rejigged as mountain ducks
on sandbars
          dugouts
              saplings
planted out
up on the hill where native growth
isn't rekindling

            navigate via call
of male white-winged triller,
loss-win ratio of northerly gusts

Upstage redbacks
snatch at prey, a nuclear test
        border test
that opens debate new mines new policies
of nation-making — conservatism
        the slower application
of extremism, clearing
to revegetate all scapes
        with poplars and Tasmanian bluegums

I smell fuel through the steel jerrycan,
degraded land of building.

Watch out : edge of storm,
perched, metal casing, locust hoppers lulled
before the flying; temporal thunder
to swallow light and colour,
phages in polished places

                                        black-faced cuckoo shrike predates
through mulberry tree, to think
I might have a revelation in mind
when I deck out Comus
in new rayon garb

I have only ever read Paradise Lost, that's true,
not a single word of anything else — or, rather,
Paradise Lost is all that's lodged,
all that's taken root,
and words sprung up
in trans-national vocabs
are derivations of what's enclosed

I tell the student my grandmother repeopled the ghost town
of her childhood, I tell her windows are the claims
of civilisation, having safe prospect; I tell her towns
in the goldfields and Pilbara
aren't just there for extraction,
but perpetual colonisation —
never believe a white guy
with a can of beer
                and a porno
playing on his dvd;
                    thunder is intense
and I was about to record lightning as a no-show,
a freaky aberration,
                but lightning is exploding
letter by letter
on the manual typewriter — the physical
exertion, stress on finger joints,
a violent arthritis of the heavens.

November. Shiny green growth
of eucalypts, late spring burst to link
little moisture around — even now the storm is sparing
in its downpour — and heat; humidity
drives the sparkle of growing tips,
flowerings?

                I need to participate,
I need the risk of being struck,
burnt to a crisp
by lightning, this devotion that forgets God
in the rush

and that's a pity, as there'll be no redrafting,
no second or third takes.

Expression of requiem pain
on the unstable imprint.

Driving through loss, deletions
every week more, though satellites incorrectly
routed over, or images
in a mass of data;

                          behind every veneer of trees
a suburb, a road widening
                          cessation
of privateering transport
and down loss ambience,
anxiety passed with sleep

but who wants to hear that?
Who wants to be reminded,
wants to deny rearranging surfaces, or
miles deep, through crust to mantle, as long as enough weight and spin
retain a planetary shape?

degrees of technology
despite the windbreak of granite,
leeward habitats exult in shelter

                                I pray compulsively,
always just before sleep and again if I wake during the night
in case I forgot before sleep

I never feel refreshed after sleep;
the blue-tongued lizard would stay inside
my head if left to it.

It's not order I look for in Tracy's eyes.

Between the transparent and the opaque
shapes compile and disperse,
a breakdown in sense reception: lethargy
is the concrete floor of the shed stained with oil
heating up — the vapours;

                         it's not even an odour,
it clogs the intake, inhalation, even through the mouth;

after the warnings and the facts, what will be left?
Should have taken notice or not been reminded,
look ahead — we
biological agents.
                 Spread.
                     Roland Barthes'
margarine scenario — true, Tracy, true. Nuttelex
(which he didn't know about… surely?)
is a vegan table spread. Literally,
maybe Barthes literally
believed in the efficacy of butter. Breton
came from butter space: poverty and wetnursing,
a differing hierarchy…

purple flowers of Paterson's curse
dry blue, giddiness in crucifix
and preface

                 patrons scaled written
what is written, copyists and calligraphers

I do not tap, as fork rake hoe axe saw shovel
leant up within
crimp of steelwork

telegraph singularly tasked wandoo pole, bolt and insulator:
to lower error rate with long passages unchecked

who to keep an eye out?

Viridescent blue beetle flies into hot metal,
inshade though superheated
curtain; a redback pauses

driving late last night no swarms of locusts — shutdown
with cool air, light-lack; it is hot today and they are manically reactivated,
each space flown from filled in by another.

Pervasive.
            Peritextual?
Browsed, though dependent on mirrors
and memory of Milton: regained, like extraterrestrial
entrepreneurial zest.
                        That's Western Australia for you,
all extrusion and removal.
                        There are thermometers everywhere
here: in the house, on the veranda, in the shed. It is compulsive;

so the sun activates flight
and agitates towards any green — surface, texture, content;

I'm only left with myself to worship from: ray out
like martyrdom, Isoscelesian in the shed;

it's a focus upwards, like the pain
that begins in my head and fluctuates with sugar
levels;

        on the bowsaw the blade is a set of four triangles
followed by a sharpened incisor, triangled out contrary to jag
and substantiate the tear;

cutter teeth (by four)
per raker tooth //

gully fill and tension

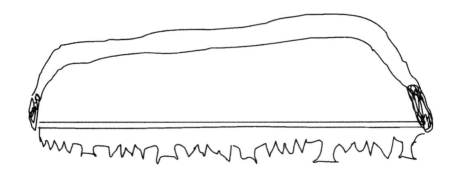

Light and vibration conjure
explosive movement: I levitate
above volcanic openings
of red ant colony, this lifting of what's deeper down
out into the open — a surge, convulsion;
it's cooler below the surface, bare and open
to the sun so close it singes
the stilled;

warmed in comorbidity
the media came yesterday to view
the flying: on the wing, clouds of locusts
stripping crops as they propel south
towards stuttering green;

ants red across everything
and report back;

abridgement depositions
temper tacit borders: we agree
tolerance in agronomies, mounds of grain
growing on swept floors, though not
fumigation, front-end loaders scooping
against the gradient/s;

                    I don't own a fingerprint,

here, ants walking over the page are not surrealist
here, a deadly spider predating above words is not surrealist
here, locusts swarming like diacriticals are not surrealist
here, snakes distracting and causing a line break are not surrealist

myth is plangent and visceral; fences sunder narrative

the eucalypt fruits pop their hoodies, sub-genre
of hip-hop where birds crosstalk

high cloud movement semi-unsettles, what's caught-up
or deflected back into atmosphere, ultra altitude
logistics of reflection, mirrors working differently,
distortion relative, fixed point
ending always in gravity, memories of…

this strabismus of perception,
placid incendiary desire

to maintain like Freud's butchery of eels and what might be
revealed

and so, the contrails nightly in colder climes

taking articles out of groupings, a set less its own,
out of the millions of locusts in the swarm
the redback spider concentrates on one only

and so, each plant a necropolis
to its own species and so 'species' clutches
evolutionary and creationist museums
arrived at complete, struggling aberrations
my long overlooking
perplexes the bobtail goanna, or it waits
to break the gaze and be shot of me;
but there's little
or no room for anathema
for votes cast apart
from shine of wattle;
no drugs keep time stilled
fait accompli, trivial
pursuit

so stuck on mutual aid, so ready and willing to assist
when the harvest is less than adequate

my contact with town
is minimal, in avoiding
it's not that I don't
want contact: Tracy
tells me what's happening

as she's often in town, steering
her way around gossip;

                straightedge

and so, they party in the Church of Christ hall, floor for hire,
across the river sermons shudder pleasantly,
avoiding the apocalyptic, cut and dried seasons
prayed for, selective as science

violence cloned from embryos, stem cell research
on the sidetracks
                cultural ban order fire danger funerals

gather privacy and gallery family to thread on trails
from far out of elsewhere, yesterday I will arrive tomorrow,
so give that a column in the newspaper
at least to identify

                I see small humanoid creatures
scuffle at dusk, swooped by owls and frogmouths,
cluttering stubble and rockfaces,
rending jam trees, making jam blood
for nightmares

                I am tired every day now
from little or less sleep — worn down with nightmaring,
who I might be

stumble through calendar and sickness, patina
of subcreativity

agitation of disbelief

there is no darkness, there are degrees of light —
light and less light and light so absent
we ruminate darkness; a dance is light like calling love
Godly: a synthesis as confronting as shade
in extreme heat   crime modulates the body temperature
                   crime takes light from the flower
                   at the precise moment of pollination
                   so caught up in aphorism a calm distracts
and the header comb strikes quartz and sparks and fire
runs through wheat like Crete where fire has left
earth bare so it is here, bare of scrub
that grows when there is only night-moisture
on a breeze that begins and ends interior,
where sun kills much that comes from elsewhere; merciless.

In such utopias I am the magpie
waiting for its mate to lift from the road,
be resurrected, body reconstituted,
soul rejoined, piping laconic fugues

                                        the locusts have stripped
silverbeet, grapevines, gnawed at capsicum seedlings

the female redback on the ironwork near where I type
has finished inducing and siphoning
the locust wrapped in her web — leaving
an emptied exoskeleton, a powerful hopping leg —
she is distinctly plumper and her red stripe
brighter

the sea breeze condenses : locusts settle in bands and patches
of oscillating frequency

                      delimited, hyperbole roughs
                      flooded gum canopy and birdcall

            quashed, participants uninterested
            or excluded; in the rush of tones
            leaves rain down on the shed roof

Luminous day sees streams of locusts
hurtling sunwards, portions of moebius strips
unravelling; from the radiator foil
you pull impacted and sliced bodies — the terror
of give as thoraxes and legs tear
away: an abjection that runs
through an appalling engagement
of soul, pragmatic disengagement
of repetition; they are dead, you say, and discard
them gently, then systematically.
Cars contradict living; core of downfall;
endgame of paradise.

And so, robust in God and omnific word
I trawl the golden compass across infra-red
radar, like Giles weather station near the Northern Territory
border
            set up to monitor British tests
at Emu Plain and Maralinga
                                    outpost
on nomadic trails.

Tempting, fruit to eat: mulberry clusters
severed by locusts and heat; Tarantula Nebula
remembers, forgets; to plat rods and cones,
bring immensity into play, let fall
so far, or touch
                    eyes closed

then not at all;

torments of virtue and bliss
like tardive dyskinesia / doxology
fleshed, tracks through forests only tangible
at night: photons rushing in and too much light,
restoratives to compel aubades,
voluble, centred by touch…

Today: jumping spider on keys of typewriter.
White-tailed spider (arachnogenic necrosis?) on pillow slip.
Climbing higher we aged faster.
Light years, an imprecise measurement.
Distortion of stars on the edge of the mirror,
Focal length of Gabriel. Omne efficiens agit
secundum vires recipientis, non suas…
Scanning the night sky. Equatorially tracking.

A fact depletes the soothsaying. Encased
within the shed, it's an insect world and a world of arachnids.
There is no visible living plantlife within: abundant
without, insects and spiders come in to nest, hunt.
I watch a daddy long-legs meticulously stalk
a massive redback. The same redback
I have been watching for days.
A bull-nosed skink and a centipede.
Rodents bringing seeds in.

All music is locked in one word, and that word
has no language. Light is syllogism.
The tint on my glasses changes.
I am no further than the glare
that hobbled me earlier.

They worked on atomic weapons

then felt guilty. Bully for them.
Our hearts bleed.

Milton Friedman just died. Old Man of Chicago School
economics. HIS economics. He never felt guilty,
I don't think, never apologised. To my knowledge.

The Treasurer deploys violence
to thwart violence, saying of protestors
at the G20 summit: 'they think they're political
but they're really criminal,'
and that's why binary stars co-exist,
why mythologies are obsessed
with reflection/s.

Free will is a drop in temperature,
not suncream applied to already
damaged skin. Melaleuca flowers
crumble: stabat mater
of brushes.

Evening and the constant flow of locusts
has been shut off — a fuse blown, flow of electrons
dampened, quashed. Walking over dead and crushed
grass, stubs of oats not even amounting to stubble,
still a flutter of locust bio-electrical impulse:
but all legs with solar panel wings
closed up, angel hoards without purpose
or target. Their stillness a requiem
for the wheatbelt, gnawed down to its monoculture,
its confusion of toxins.
                              Here, there are globes
of Venus and Mars, earth's moon,
so intricately marked, profiled. The gaps
are filled in, mission by mission.
The earth itself is missing. A soul-less orrery.
Ants are fast-tracking as the sun dips:
breaking up locusts into segments, bits
transferable through their holes,
into their tunnels. Their larders

are grotesquely replete — a tussle
with inheritance. So reliant on gravity,
on the revolutions per hour
of the earth's spin. Their hosts
proclaiming solemn council:
                heat and light,
sun's expansion and contraction,
last hurrah.

They will come in the garb of heaven and promise
longevity for the planet;
They will come as scientists telling us what is good for us,
deleting all choice;
They will sup with the string-pullers;
They will take us to the nethermost abyss and shilly shally
on borders of light;
They will commission their poets and artists and musicians
to commemorate, reconcile intangibles.

           Respect a disclaimer
        all overuse is, seeing the comet
           more visibly through binoculars
        than a Newtonian reflector — damn thing
           also needs mirror coated and polished
        and brought back into alignment.

Cradle, Babel, I collect hairs moulted
from my temples and place them in my top
shirt pocket —
           I fear the use they might put it to,
curses that might be flung. An innocent shedding
in a taxi, a library, caught up in someone else's crime,
narrative plotting.
           Filed as conclusive.

I leave traces of blood nowhere
and recoil from contact with anything that might be
the blood of another.
                                Intactness.
The sun sunk the serpent sleeps — I clutch
my Milton closer.
                        The thought of false accusation
makes me quiver.
                        I don't mind being hated.

'Of evil then, so small, as easy think
The remedy: perhaps more valid arms,
Weapons more violent...'
                                They don't go out, in case
a sliver of self is shed.

                                Intactness.

What do you wear when tremors upset the steel frame of the house?
What do you consume when lightning knocks out the power?
What do you pray when cataclysm is so loud
you can't hear yourself think?

                        Prayer needs... zip?

The mouth of the bull-ants' nest up behind the shed
is massive — a gaping maw you could insert
two or three digits in without damaging the stick-built sides:
you know bull-ants would rip your flesh apart
and fill you with enough formic acid
to make your eyes run acid tears.
You wouldn't disturb them anyway.
And your soul is alkaline
by way of back-up.

And so to whirl the shale,
plates settled as complementaries
and superstitions — don't tempt
monopolies and cartels on a fiercely
hot day, mosquitoes drawn

And so, horoscopes of shale
compress before it began to renounce
cascading electricity — between the sheets — dead leaves
reaching the crowns of marri —
fresh tips whipping in the west wind.

                              As a toddler I was encircled
by the dissolution of clocks — cogs, gears, wheels — springs
so delicate producing more energy than seemed allowable: something
stored in them longer. I thought in formulas,
but you don't have to believe that.

                    Dehydrated, I want to sweat more.
                    The redback survived the daddy long-legs'
                              assault —
                    fool, I had given it up to juxtapositions
                    and death. SO, theorists of poetry
                    say change and redirection are politically
                    good, defensible. Narcissism is the child
                    of invention. We speak out against
                              governments
                    and foreign policy. We live to die another
                              day.
                    And still attend the movies. Tracy is correct:
                    the extreme heat of the 23rd November 2006,
                    just outside York, Western Australia,
                    at the foot of Walwalinj, has brought out
                    the bull-nosed skinks, double-plus.
                    Book and movie made profound
                              impressions
                    on me as a youth. I dreamed of being

                    among the wattles and eucalypts,
                    and elsewhere.

          Ample world?

Horses out of the apocalypse
take what's taken — open roads
where flooded gums offer roost
to white-faced herons, egrets,
ringnecked parrots, crows, willy wagtails,
doves, corellas in vast white-out flocks,
galahs enmeshed with static, kookaburras,
wattle birds, honey-eaters, flycatchers — rebuff
the liminal so expansive in riff and rift,
states of profiteering.

Regazetted. Equine precinct. Racing money.
'They've got pots of money and will hit with a big stick.'

          They'll come with bulldozers and bridle trails
and make lifestyle decisions as neat as white fences,
wonderland — as if they care for horses
or the magnificent concentrations of corellas
coiled through the district

                              the storm last night so violent
it made appliances spit warnings — weight of rain
anomalous but as insistent as the Pearl poet's obsession
with cleanness

                    and so, hoodwinked into contact,
                    we become glass to developers,
                    clear even at twilight, rotation
                    of all planted places

          The young bungarra goanna skated across surface,
head held high, broad-chested over the bank

I will lay myself down before the bulldozers
I will believe my resistance the resistance of all animals and plants
I will not let the wealthy and their shire-stooges make hay,
       their horses performing for investors
I will continue watering tree seedlings, drinking less myself
I will die with abuse pouring from my lips

And this troubles me.

Two Chosen Broadsheet Poets

Caroline Clark and Adam Wyeth

Caroline Clark, 30, comes from Lewes in Sussex. After graduating with a degree in German and Russian from Exeter University, she moved to Moscow where she lived for 8 years. In 2002 she completed an MA in Modern European Literature at Sussex University, and wrote her dissertation on Paul Celan and Osip Mandelstam. She now lives in Montreal.

The Myth of the Nightingale

For Moscow

Arrowshadowed I wait at the city's core,
earthbound in dust. First murmurs an underground
stream, gurgling audible waterways, sound
becoming beaded globes propelled through narrow
canals. When away is all I know – now break
these ambersounded notes. All of me is burgeoning
to burst these boulders, pebbles and stones and over-
flow, flower into the kerbside world.

All that you hear is real. May you be blessed
in strangeness, loved in newness. I'll shake you loose
a summer storm against the background roar.
Through jasmine and lime, I'll sing you to my source.
Let there be flowers in the sand, lilacs in the streets,
I can make more life, more life than the sun.

Tonight Moscow

when your streets are beyond
the touch of sun,
and darkness gulfs your greying gullies,
let your rooftops flare red,
flank by flank
each stand of white.

From shadow streets to desert fire
your heights to where the railway track
cuts through a depth now full with light,
one second acres wide
set with stones of paradise –
Moscow flare red tonight.

Tale of Tales

And then I came to a place
where the tower blocks stop
and do not give way to woods
or open field. They end in the edge
of their ending. They stop.

I had set off like many before
in autumn. Underfoot a mishmash
of leaves. First came potholes,
things to avoid, obscenities.
Or was it gestures – a tugging

at comprehension? First came the word.
They took me to a village wedding,
the name of the place meant apples.
Yábloka, yábloka. Give me a word
I can understand. Say it with a bite.

Here is only memory giving up
its silence. Later alone come crunching
through snow, come in from the cold with frost
on your clothes smelling of yellowing
apples. These words are not my own.

Apples, Russian apples, the year's
late harvest remembered. Buy
a bucket of my finest, ever so
sour, the best. And here's a sprig
of flowering dill, just for you.

Like the ghost of a song at night
may your home return to you.
If you forget the words
you'll remember the tune.
Turn back before it's too late.

A is for apple, *ya* is for *yábloko.*
The jaw, the cheek, where both
can meet. Difference – a place between
tongue and teeth. Say it with a bite.
    Say it until you get it right.

Dacha

i

They wait
in white expectation,

a tablecloth
tatters in the sun,

minutes long gone
circle like flies,

and still the blank-eyed days
push on through the taiga.

ii

Mosquitoes descend
at twilight,

cups accumulate
saying when,
hours tag
the stork's crooked flight,

and the rocking chair
deepens its grooves
trying, trying to remember.

iii

Absent visitors
long gone

a cloth
tatters

they wait
in white

memories
circle.

Adam Wyeth, 29, is originally from Sussex but now lives in Co. Cork. His poems have been published in numerous literary journals, including *Magma, Poetry London, The Stinging Fly, The Shop* and *Southword* (Ireland). He has been anthologized in the O'Brien Press award winning anthology *Something Beginning with P* and was a runner-up in the last Arvon International Poetry Competition.
He has been selected for the *Poetry Ireland* Introductions Series in Dublin, (2007). He is Director of WORD UP! poetry readings, under the auspices of Kinsale Arts Week. He has also made two films on poetry: *A Life in A Day of Desmond O'Grady,* first screened at the Cork Film Festival, 2004; and *Soundeye*: Cork International Poetry Festival, 2005. He teaches Creative Writing in Cork.

Leland Bardwell

night I could not sleep
I came to read you in lamplight –
poking out the rushes
of books, festooned on my shelves
that I look upon as family.
But Leland, you were the least familiar
of kith and kin, given me
by your son, Nicholas in Dingle.
And so, Leland Bardwell,

I stretched out your pages like arms
and undressed you
with my eyes, my ears, my nose, my hands,
my mouth – watering inside –
devoured you! Night I could not sleep,
Leland Bardwell
I came to you out of the rushes of bed sheets,
and held your slender spine
tenderly as the first time I found poetry
singing in me.
The lines of your life on Lower Leeson Street
opened and closed like doors
in my mind, and the sun and moon rose
at the same time.
Leland Bardwell, night I could not sleep
I came to raise the dead
weight of my head from its rushes of knots
and lay it on your lap
where your lyrics ran like fingers through my locks.
Night cannot contain
the strain of thoughts that fly between these walls –
so I have come
to settle them in words –
plucking them
from the air, where all things come.
Such thoughts
I had while reading you Leland Bardwell,
night I could not sleep.

Carry The Torture

Today I must remember
to email my father,
who has a tumour
the size of a cucumber
growing in his liver.

It came like a whisper
by text from my sister.
She says he's in good humour
but I'm sure he'd rather
not suffer chemo all summer.

Truth is, he's known all winter,
felt it growing bigger,
tried to keep it under,
till it jutted from his figure
like the Dingle peninsula.

Only then did he call the doctor.
My dad, who thinks he's bigger
than life – who never bothers
to lift his finger and dial my number,
who told me not to whimper

when I was a wee nipper,
who gave me the cold shoulder,
is now looking for a shoulder
to cry on. I could raise my finger,
but now I've grown older,

I no longer carry the torture.
It's him that's grown bitter,
and like a witch doctor
has taken the disorder
down into his liver –

spreading like a rumour.

Chamber Music

The one piece of music that churns my stomach
is Schubert's Quintet in C

since my grandmother told me
this is what Nazi officers played full volume

to drown out the moans of millions of Jews
as they were led into those rooms.

No matter how stirring a pitch the violins reach,
or how heavily the plangent cellos sigh –

I see their gaunt naked forms fall like flies
in a poisonous fog; reduced to cow pat

lining the floors, then shit-shovelled into pits
while the whole movement plays over and again

never reaching the end, like a scratched record
that keeps jumping back.

Dad

I'll always remember those Sunday drives home.
How a blackening silence came over us
with the night. I'd look back at the road
we set out on when our weekend had begun:

singing songs, stopping at petrol stations
in the back of beyond, turning off the beaten
track and finding a pub for lunch –
with swings and climbing frames to play on.

But all that was fading fast, as signs marked
the dwindling miles, oncoming headlights
dazzled us, the final catseyes blinked past
and the road emptied – losing its nerve

as we curved off the motorway. Then the real
darkness set in – and the chill of parting
made me numb. I'd run upstairs to my room
without a word spoken, and out the corner

of my window watch your silver Citroen slip
into the night; a final sliver of light then total eclipse.
Another week of staring into space in classrooms,
waiting for our next outing all together. Save mum.

Notes for Broadsheet Poets 10

Many poets compose poems about the actual writing of a poem. Here are a few examples that came in recently.

In this poem, with its assonantal (vowel) end rhymes, **Ann Leahy**, who lives in Dublin, writes about an 'unknown poem' which relates to the 'unknown poem' of Auden, extracts from which feature in these **Notes** later. Ann's poems have won many prizes and awards and she has appeared in several anthologies.

Wishing Lines

I put words down along a line
Hoping for a turn of phrase
That will whisk them off and away
To snatch a sigh from a telegraph wire,

Catch a burble of a broken main,
A patch of sunlight from a two-tiered
Interchange, swirl them back to me,
Trailing a whiff of mugwort, a trace

Of old man's beard, and carrying an overtone
Of something I haven't yet pegged down.

I think a lot of poets would identify with the way **Amy Handler** suggests we can never actually own the words we use in her poem, 'Artistic Process'. The language has a life of its own   This recalls, perhaps at a tangent, a memorable line from **Auden**: 'Words have no word for words that are not true'.

It also brings to mind **MacNeice**'s amusing 'Elegy for Minor Poets' who were 'the world's best talkers' but 'as writers lacked a sense of touch'. So they 'either gave up or just went on and on – /Let us salute them now their chance is gone...' The following two lines apply to poets whether unknown, minor or major:

Let the sun clamber onto the notebook, shine,
And fill in what they groped for in each line.

Amy lives in Brookline, Massachusetts. She writes short stories also and makes films. This is her first poem to be published.

Artistic Process

Today I awake with pieces of poetry in my head.
Just like that they are there
Though I don't dream them this way.
Not quite awake I scribble them down
Before they become something else.

Is this how it is for you too?
Do your words arrive in a flash
Demanding to be written?

Now that I'm thinking, I'll put these words aside
And continue them later when I'm not.
Then the seeds of verse can rest to re-awaken me.

See how I never call them 'my' words?
This is because those un-thought never belong to me.
They live on their own
From beginning to end
While I tag along with my pen.

All poets are readers whether of their own pages, the work of others, of situations, of people, of landscapes, of the skies, of sounds, sights, textures and touches. And, of course, any single poem becomes a million different poems according to the million different readings by readers.

*

The distinguished poet/critic, **Tom Paulin** offers a fresh, original approach to untapping the secret 'codes' of poems in his very recently published Poetry Primer: *The Secret Life of Poems* (Faber £17.99 hardback, 2008). He explained: 'I wanted to write a book which would be about the DNA structure of poetry. The way poets talk about poetry in terms of rhythm and metre and cadence... I think in terms of images or rhythms and I had the idea of writing what I hoped would be a kind of handbook.' In this stimulating resource for both writers of poetry and readers, Paulin takes forty-seven examples from throughout the ages, from Milton and Wordsworth to Auden and Heaney, and gives his unique interpretation of how he sees poetry working through the chosen poems. It was during his own reading of a poem by Yeats that he 'began to imagine a critical account of his or any poet's work which jettisoned all earnest explication of the text and concentrated on sound, cadence, metre, rhyme, form.' Conventional critical analysis of a poem is thus thrown out of the window and Paulin uncovers a finer coded structure behind the obvious structure of a poem. He articulately concentrates on a poem's acoustic memory composed of intricate sound patterns that constitute a kind of subtext of meaning. To do this, he scans, dissects syllables, and interprets shifting rhythms and their inferences. He shows himself to be a penetrating historian who illuminates, through the sound patterns in a particular poem, the historical and political contexts that the poet may or may not be conscious of. Seen through his eyes, a poem can be saying much more than it appears to say behind images in the surface text; sounds, images, style as well as tone constitute a kind of code – often political and linked to a certain anxiety – and can say at times even more than the said, articulating on occasions what, maybe for political, religious or moral reasons, cannot actually be recorded at the time.

Paulin's approach to each poem is humble (he prefaces most of his points with 'perhaps', 'maybe', or 'it may be that', avoiding didacticism and acknowledging that these are only his propositions), and also almost visionary:

What had always seemed to me an imperfect poem changed when I began to write about it and an altogether finer structure started to reveal itself.

Paulin might be a little wild at times in his illuminations e.g. on John Montague's 'All Legendary Obstacles': 'The guttural *k* in the pejorative "ruck" is magnified by the guttural in "obstacles". It's an untidy, scrummy word, "ruck", not too far from "fuck"'. Or, listen to this – on Robert Browning's 'Meeting at Night', referring to the lines: …'the quick sharp scratch/And blue spurt of a lighted match' which, to the uninitiated seems to be just what it says:

This is the fire of passion, the spurt of male orgasm, the quick of life, but she is in control here. Having coded intense longing and desire to this point, the poem has nowhere else to go.

He continues to get a little carried away. The lake in Robert Frost's 'A Servant to Servants' is 'virginal' and could be 'an unstained bedsheet'; a notch cut in wood is 'a threatening phallic image', 'but the effect is vaginal, though dry and negative (the word contains "not" which can also be read as "knot", representing marriage…)' Later in the same poem, what seems to be a plain, ordinary 'book of ferns', according to Paulin, 'brings pubic hair somewhere into the image'.

Apart from such dubious claims as those just mentioned, Paulin seems very sound and plausible. He stresses 'the redemptive nature of metre' and how 'poetry begins in speech, in the skipping rhymes and chants children make up in the playground and the street' and then moves through various stages 'from oral tradition, communal memory, into print'. He adds interesting little anecdotes such as 'that most hermetic and difficult of symbolist poets', Mallarmé, teaching his school pupils English nursery rhymes to the 'great anger' of a school inspector in 1880. He recounts that 'Dryden knew that the English Language depends on the struggle between monosyllabic and polysyllabic words'. He even seems to indulge in an insider's gossip when he imparts with relish the fate of Keith Douglas's stormy affair with Antoinette Beckett who married a highly decorated South African pilot and became active in Black Sash, a group of women who silently protested against apartheid. She ended her relationship with him when she decided she could stand his jealousy no longer, and died in Warwick aged seventy nine.

Paulin adds a fresh, lively vocabulary to poetry criticism, speaking of 'broken-backed lines', of a line 'drawing attention to itself', of Donne 'flogging the s sound', of Hopkins 'deliberately smashing' the rhythms, of a line being 'keyed' to the speaking voice, of what 'drives' opening lines, of internal rhyme 'boxing in' the subject, of the line being 'oiled by noun particles', of ' a deliberate push of the pen nib, its black ink seeding the last particle', of an 'annoying susurrus', of rhymes 'clicking shut', of adjectives being 'cleansed' of the 'effort' of the first few lines, of creating 'unhurried space for the unaccompanied human voice', of an o serving 'to fur the vowel', of 'a military push' taking place in lines that are forced up, of 'choke-bands', of language as being 'highly strung', and 'the life of language' depending on the poet's handling of it. He points out that exclamation marks should not be used flippantly, that the pace of dashes should be considered. He alerts us to the need for pauses which have their own special powers such as creating and enforcing authority, preventing a 'couplet from sounding glib', 'containing and expressing desire, or signifying rejection' as they 'follow the rhythms of the speaking voice':

Poems depend on rhythms, but they also need pauses, sometimes deep pauses, that say more than words or rhythms can, and remind us that silence can state its own meaning.

Paulin is daring enough to choose some poems ignored by critics, such as Robert Frost's 'The Investment', and to choose other famous poems he considers no good. For example, in focusing on 'Musée des Beaux Arts' by **Auden**, he admires the intimate tender opening that 'puts the poet and the reader on an equal communicative level', and he mines into what the poem suggests in its subtext, finding political meanings in the adjectives, and coupling biographical and historical perspectives. Yet he ends up consigning it, in the poem's words, as ' "an interesting failure" by a writer who went on to become quite an important failure, writing poems in a glossy, metropolitan, intellectually inflected language that read rather like chirpy opinion pieces in the *New Yorker*'.

John Fuller, the eminent Auden scholar and poet, would not agree. In his fine 613-page *W.H. Auden: A Commentary* (Faber 1998), he appraises the poem: 'This is one of Auden's most celebrated short poems. Its long irregular lines create an illusory casualness of argument, which the rhymes subtly enforce'...

Paulin is far less harsh on **Louis MacNeice** and his poem 'Order to View' which he sets in its historical context and comments on its 'spreading pattern of internal rhymes', influenced by Irish poetry. He continues to demonstrate how repeated sounds such as 'en', 'ih', and 'o' conjure both the atmosphere and meaning, and concludes in the typical style of the virtuoso that he is:

That *ih* sound so dominant in the middle stanza, is cleanly revived in the last line's 'windows', which contains the verb 'win' (the consonant *n* draws out the vowel). The *oh* sound furred by *s* is repeated in 'windows', but MacNeice bats *o* out again in the very last word 'open', where the plosive *p* stretches the sound out and lifts it up. We hear 'hope' in 'open', so this is a victorious line – demoralisation and dullness have been cast off.

Tom Paulin's singlemindedness and dedication is an example to all young poets. When he started writing poetry seriously in 1972, he would get up at seven o'clock every morning and write for an hour before going to his teaching job. As a lad of 16 or 17, he was inspired by Robert Frost's use of the vernacular. 'He taught you to respect the way people around you spoke'. A point worth listening to. And an idea to read your own poem out loud because you can then pick out the bits that don't flow, where you stumble or run out of breath. You know then where the poem needs more work.

*

In **Auden's 'Unwritten Poem', 'Dichtung und Wahrheit'** there are gems of advice for young poets:

> Of any poem written by someone else, my first demand is that it be good; of any by myself, my first demand is that it be genuine, recognizable, like my handwriting, as having been written, for better or worse, by me. (When it comes to his own poems, a poet's preferences and those of his readers often overlap but seldom coincide.)

> The poem which I should now like to write would not only have to be good and genuine: if it is to satisfy me, it must also be true.

To Auden, recognising the poem as 'genuine' is like recognising the poet's 'handwriting'. He stresses that one has to come under the 'syllabic spell' of a poem.

> As an Artistic language, Speech has many advantages – three persons, three tenses (Music and Painting have only the Present Tense), both the active and the passive voice – but it has one serious defect: it lacks the Indicative Mood. All its statements are in the subjunctive and only possibly true until verified (which is not always possible) by non-verbal evidence.

Auden concludes this sequence by describing the 'unwritten poem':'words cannot verify themselves. So this poem will remain unwritten.'

*

Nanos Valaoritis, a celebrated Greek poet, now aged 86, knew **MacNeice, Auden** and **Chester Kallman**, and his fascinating memoir can be read on the website (www.agendapoetry.co.uk) in the supplement to this **Lauds** issue (essay section).

The following two poems from one of Nanos's poetry collections, *Pan Daimonium* (Philos Press, Washington, 2005), illustrate beautifully how everyone, even well-known poets such as Nanos, has unwritten poems in them.

Untitled

For many years I have pursued a poem
Which regularly escapes me
It's a funny little poem
About nothing at all
If I remember well
Such as those written today
And cleverly crafted to say nothing
Yet this little poem became a hole
In my life: a small black hole
Out of which poured nothingness
And – invaded me, slowly
With its deadly darkness
While I stood there steadfast
Holding on for dear life
To the sinking twilight
And now it's too late
To remember anything
About this empty spot
This grain of something greater
Than anything in the universe.

Every Night I Dream

Every night I dream of great poetry
Quite different from mine
Or what I will ever write
And yet – every night I dream
Of this very different poetry
Composed of lines so solid
So dense and grainy
They could have been made of granite
I ask myself – what is their subject
What do they say these marvellous lines
Which to behold – will leave you aghast

They'll take your breath away
But – however – in any case – I'm sorry to say
Impossible to guess what it's all about
And I have tried and tried, believe me,
And puzzled over these lines
Day after day – and in the night
They keep on coming back
With new earthshaking and tremendous
Messages – of great import
That everyone should hear
But not a single word remains
When I open my eyes – they're gone
They vanish in pure daylight
These huge edifices – those titanic
Workings of each night.

These **Notes** were written and compiled by **Patricia McCarthy**

Marie Wilson, the wife of Nanos Valaoritis
and a celebrated artist, was a close friend of
the surrealist **André Breton**, **Man Ray** and
Picasso. She also met **Auden** and **MacNeice**.
Her colourful paintings can be seen on the
website: www.agendapoetry.co.uk

Biographies

Erinn Batykefer earned her MFA from the University of Wisconsin-Madison and is currently the Stadler Poetry Fellow at Bucknell University where she is Associate Editor of *West Branch*. Her poetry and creative non-fiction have appeared in such journals as *Gulf Coast, Prairie Schooner, Maisonneuve Magazine,* and *Threepenny Review,* among others.

Linda Benninghoff has been published in *The London Times Online, Erbacce* and other magazines. She has published two chapbooks, *Departures* and *The Street Where I Was a Child.* She translated *The Seafarer* from Anglo-Saxon; the translation appears online at **www.electrato.com** under Dialogue of Nations Through Translation

Diana Brodie is a New Zealander living in Cambridge. Her work was included in the anthology, *Entering the Tapestry* and two poems were winners in the Poetry Society's Members' Competitions. Poems have also appeared, or are soon to appear, in *Smith's Knoll, The Interpreter's House, Quattrocento* and *Poetry Nottingham.* She is currently working on her first collection.

Norman Buller was educated at Fircroft College, Birmingham and St. Catharine's College, Cambridge. His verse has been widely published in the U.K. and abroad. Two poetry collections *Travelling Light* (2005) and *Sleeping with Icons* (2007) – are both available from Waterloo Press, 126 Furze Croft, Hove BN3 1PF.

Greg Delanty is the Artist in Residence at St. Michael's College, Vermont. His *Collected Poems 1986-2006* is recently out from Carcanet Press. His other more recent books are *The Ship of Birth* (Carcanet Press 2003), *The Blind Stitch* (Carcanet Press 2001) and *The Hellbox* (Oxford University Press 1998)). Greg Delanty has received numerous awards and has just been granted a Guggenheim Fellowship for Poetry.

Roger Elkin has over forty years' experience of teaching English Literature primarily to adults on a range of courses in Further Education. He is also a prize-winning poet; he currently has seven collections in print, and at least four looking for a home.

John Gibbens won an Eric Gregory Award in 1982. He published a *Collected Poems* in 2000 and *The Nightingale's Code: a poetic study of Bob Dylan* in 2001. He works as a journalist in London, was deputy editor of *The Oldie* for a while, and is now a casual sub. 'Shelf-Life', an occasional column about secondhand book hunting, appears occasionally in the *Sunday Telegraph.* Further poems, songs and drawings at www.touched.co.uk.

Rüdiger Görner is Professor of German at Queen Mary University of London, and founding Director of the Centre for Anglo-German Cultural Relations. Between 1999 and 2004 he was Director of the Institute of Germanic Studies and founded the Ingeborg Bachmann Centre for Austrian Literature. His main research areas comprise representations of science and music in the German language literatures, from the late eighteenth century to the present day, poetic theory at the turn of the centuries, the literary aesthetics of repetition and the conception of pluralectics in German (late) Romanticism. He has published studies on Hölderlin's poetics, the Goethezeit, Austrian Literature from Stifter to Thomas Bernhard, on Rilke, and on Thomas Mann and his notion of finality in culture. His publications are too numerous to list.

Wolfgang Görtschacher is an Assistant Professor at the University of Salzburg. He is the author of *Little Magazine Profiles: The Little Magazines in Great Britain 1939-1993* (1993) and *Contemporary Views on the Little Magazine Scene* (2000). He is the owner-director of the press Poetry Salzburg and edits *Poetry Salzburg Review*.

John Greening has published eleven collections; his latest is *Iceland Spar* (Shoestring). Winner of the Bridport Prize and the TLS Centenary Prize, he reviews poetry and music for the TLS and is a Poetry School tutor. He has just published studies of Ted Hughes and Thomas Hardy (both from Greenwich Exchange) and is preparing a book about Edward Thomas, while editing an anthology of music poems.

Nigel Jarrett is a freelance journalist and music critic, and joint winner of the Rhys Davies Award for short fiction. His work has appeared in the *Observer magazine*, *London Magazine*, *Poetry Wales*, *Agenda*, *Outposts* and many others. His stories have been anthologised in publications by London Magazine Editions, the Welsh Arts Council and Parthian. Among recent work is an essay on Delius (*Planet*) and a feature on confronting Jewish themes in fiction (*Jewish Renaissance*).

Roland John's latest poetry collection is *A Lament for England* (Bluechrome). His poems, translations, criticism and book reviews have appeared in many U.S. & U.K. journals including *Agenda*. His prose books include *A Beginner's Guide to The Cantos of Ezra Pound*. He is the publisher of the Hippopotamus Press.

Chris Jones is Lecturer in Poetry at the University of St. Andrews and a published poet. He is a specialist in Old English and his book, *Strange Likeness: The Use of Old English in Twentieth Century Poetry* was published by Oxford University Press in 2006 (and is mentioned in the Introduction to this issue).

John Kinsella is the author of many books of poetry – published by Bloodaxe, Salt and Norton – for which he has been highly praised. He divides his time between the US, Australia where he was brought up and England. He is a Fellow of Churchill College, Cambridge University, Professor of English at Kenyon College where he edits the American journal, *The Kenyon Review*, and Adjunct Professor to Edith Cowan University. His recent collections, *Peripheral Light: New and Selected Poems*, and *The New Arcadia: Poems*, both published by Norton were reviewed by Martin Dodsworth in a previous issue of *Agenda*: *Poems on Water*, Vol. 42 No.1 (£8). A book, *Disclosed Poetics: Beyond Landscape and Lyricism* was published recently in December 2007 by Manchester University Press.

Peter McDonald is a poet and critic, whose books include *Pastorals* (Carcanet, 2004), *The House of Clay* (Carcanet, 2007) and *Serious Poetry: Form and Authority from Yeats to Hill* (OUP, 2002; paperback, 2007). He is the editor of Louis MacNeice's *Collected Poems* (Faber, 2007). He works in Oxford, where he is Christopher Tower Student and Tutor in Poetry in the English Language at Christ Church College, Oxford.

Brendan McMahon is a psychotherapist, university teacher, poet and reviewer living in Derbyshire, married with two sons. His work has appeared in a wide range of magazines such as *Stand, Poetry Ireland, Ambit*, and his fourth collection, *Mythologies*, is just out from FRAS. His book on the psychology of Celtic Myth, *The Princess who Ate People*, was published recently by Heart of Albion Press.

Sam Milne lives and works in Surrey, although his heart resides in Aberdeen. He is currently writing a long essay on the Scots dialect-writer Flora Garry who writes in Broad Buchan, his own native language. He has just written a novel which is looking for a publisher, and has completed a study on Marcel Proust which will be included in his forthcoming book of collected essays. He is also updating his critical study on the poetry of Geoffrey Hill. He has no regrets about retiring from teaching!

Susan Minish was born in London, attended school in England and then Heidelburg University. She worked in London and as a governess in Spain. She has lived in the West of Ireland for the last 40 years. A number of her poems have been published, and she won first prize in the 'Crann' poetry competition in 2002.

Peter Mudford is Professor Emeritus in English and European Literature at Birkbeck College in the University of London, the author of many books and articles, most recently, *Making Theatre* (Athlone Press). His article on Auden and Kallman's writing of the libretto for Stravinsky's *The Rake's Progress* will appear in the programme book for Garsington Opera's production this summer.

Steven O'Brien grew up singing. His Welsh and Irish family were all conjurors of song. His primal poetic touchstones are the towering hymns of Wales and the muscular ballads of Ireland. He lives in Worthing and lectures in Creative Writing at the University of Portsmouth. His first full-length collection, *Dark Hill Dreams*, was published by **Agenda Editions** in 2006.

Dennis O'Driscoll's eight books of poetry include *New and Selected Poems* (Anvil Press, 2004), a Poetry Book Society Special Commendation, and *Reality Check* (Anvil Press, 2007). A selection of his essays and reviews, *Troubled Thoughts, Majestic Dreams* (Gallery Press), was published in 2001. He is editor of the *Bloodaxe Book of Poetry Quotations* (2006).

Desmond O'Grady is a well-known poet and translator with publications too numerous to mention. He is a specialist in Arabic poetry, and lives in Kinsale, Cork, Ireland.

John Powell Ward is Honorary Research Fellow at the University of Wales, Swansea. His *Selected and New Poems* appeared from Seren in 2004 and a new collection *The Last Green Year* is due from Cinnamon Press in 2009. His latest critical book is *The Spell of the Song*, Fairleigh Dickinson University Press USA.

Wendy Robinson is a Jungian psychotherapist who lives in Exeter. She was brought up on a sheep farm on the Yorkshire Moors. This is her first major publication.

Anne Ryland lives in Berwick-upon-Tweed, where she teaches adults and facilitates writing workshops. She was recently poet in residence at a home for the elderly. Her first collection, *Autumnologist*, (Arrowhead Press) was shortlisted for The Forward Prize for Best First Collection in 2006.

Geraldine Paine gained an M.Phil in Writing at the University of Glamorgan in 2000. Her poems have been published in *The Rialto, The Shop, Magma, Envoi, Soundings, The Interpreter's House, Seam, Smith's Knoll, Connections, Equinox, The New Writer, The Frogmore Papers,* the e-zine wanderingdog.com, the Kent and Sussex Competition Anthology 2000. She was shortlisted for The Cinnamon Press Poetry Collection Competition and is published in the 2007 Anthology, *Shape Sifting*.

Sue Roe is a poet, novelist and biographer who lives in Brighton. Her most recent books are *Gwen John :A Life* (Vintage) and *The Private Lives of the Impressionists* (Vintage), which has been translated into six languages. Her poetry is widely published in journals and anthologies including *New Poetries III* (Carcanet). She teaches creative writing at the University of Sussex, where she runs the MA in Creative Writing and Authorship.

Chrys Salt has been the recipient of several awards and bursaries, and had a Writers' Residency at London University. She edits the literary magazine *Markings* and is artistic director of The Bakehouse, a poetry venue in SW Scotland (**www.thebakehouse.info**) . Her first volume of poetry, *Inside Out*, was published by Autolycus in 1989 and a new collection, *Greedy for Mulberries*, will be published this Spring.

Kate Scott's first poetry collection, *Stitches*, was published by Peterloo Poets. She was commended in the collection category of the 2007 *New Writer* poetry competition. Recent poems have appeared in *The Rialto*, *Magma* and *Poetry Nottingham*.

Alex Smith who has lived in Saffron Walden since 1982, won the New Essex Writing Competition in 1993 and the London Barbican 'Blue Nose Poets of the Year' Competition for his sequence of poems, *Fenland*, in 2001. As well as appearing regularly in a wide variety of poetry magazines and literary journals, he has published four volumes of poetry including *The Appetites of Morning, the Languor of Afternoons* (1996, Salzburg University) and *Ocean Myths*, illustrated by Beatrice Brandt (Ino Press, 1999). He gained a masters degree in Creative Writing at Glamorgan University in 2001 and has taught creative writing at Essex University and Cambridge Regional College.

Will Stone, born in 1966, is a poet and translator living in Suffolk. His critical work has been published in the *TLS*, *the Guardian*, *PN Review* and *Poetry Review*. His poems have also appeared in The Wolf, The Shop, The London Magazine and Poetry Salzburg. His first collection *Glaciation* was published by Salt in 2007. *To The Silenced – Selected Poems of Georg Trakl* was published by Arc in 2005.

N S Thompson has published reviews, critical studies, translations and poetry, most recently in *Agenda*, *The Dark Horse*, *Poetry Review*, *The Reader*, *Stand* and the *TLS*. He still regrets having missed Auden's reading in Ilkley.

Andrew Waterman was born in London in 1940. After various clerical and manual jobs, he read English literature at Leicester University, and from 1968 to 1997 taught at the University of Ulster. He now lives in Norwich. His nine books of poetry include *Collected Poems* (2000) and *The Captain's Swallow* (2007), both published by Carcanet. Andrew Waterman is a recipient of the Cholmondeley Award for Poets. His website is at **www. andrewwaterman.co.uk**

John White was born and grew up in County Londonderry. He read English at Oxford, and has worked as a civil servant, teacher, and officer with Oxfordshire LEA. He recently completed the Oxford Masters degree in Creative Writing, passing with distinction. Several of his poems appeared in *Oxford Poets 2007: An Anthology* (Carcanet). He is currently working on his first collection.

Dylan Willoughby's poems have appeared recently in the online supplement to *Agenda's* Past Histories issue, as well as in *Stand* and *Shenandoah* (US) and in a broadside printed by Littoral Press. He will be a writer-in-residence at the Yaddo artists' colony in upstate New York this spring. He lived for many years in the East Village, around the corner from Auden's old apartment.

Split Stone, 1973 lithograph. Reproduced by kind permission of
The Henry Moore Foundation, and of the Artco Gallery, Leeds.

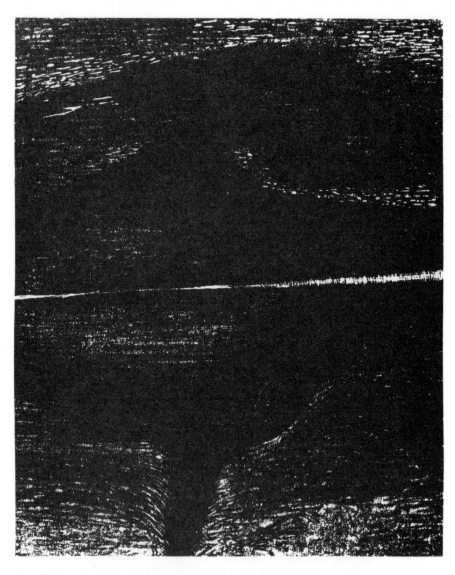

Divided Landscape, 1973 lithograph. Reproduced by kind permission of The Henry Moore Foundation, and of the Artco Gallery, Leeds.